"Discretion has been defined as the composure of speaking and behaving in such a way as to avoid causing offense. Sadly, it has been almost completely lost in our present generation. Such wise and weighty biblical axioms such as "wise as serpents and harmless as doves" and the "servant of the Lord must not be contentious, but gentle to all men" have been sorely neglected to the tune of gospel ineffectiveness. Blake Long's book, Gospel Smugness, is a timely wake up call. The author engages believers to think biblically and to act prudently in their approach to sinners and saints in our day. For those who aspire to greater efficiency in such vital works of evangelism and edification, I warmly commend this superb work."

—DON CURRIN, *Don Currin Ministries*

"The Bible instructs us to "speak the truth in love" (Ephesians 4:15). Many Christians need to be reminded that the "in love" part is just as inspired and authoritative as the "speak the truth" part. As Christians, we rightly believe in the inerrancy of scripture and the exclusivity of Jesus Christ. We have truth on our side. But we often fail to communicate that truth in love, especially in this social media age; a platform that is a rich breeding ground for un-Christlike speech. Blake Long has written an excellent and much needed book on how to boldly proclaim Christ's undiluted truth in a way that honors and pleases Him. I commend this work to you. It is a needed and timely exhortation for us all."

—JUSTIN PETERS, *evangelist, apologist, Justin Peters Ministries*

"It is so easy for us to confuse the confidence the Gospel gives us for arrogance and bravado that comes from self. Our brother has done us a magnificent service in calling us to reject fleshly confidence and return to Gospel assurance. This will be a book our church uses in its evangelism training without question!"

—KOFI ADU-BOAHEN, *Church Planter, Redeemer Bible Fellowship, Medford, OR*

"Here's a book that meets a vital need in being useful witnesses to the gospel today. While others have emphasized the necessity of faithfully proclaiming sound gospel content, or relying on the sovereign work of God for results, Blake Long's book *Gospel Smugness* stresses that we who call the world to receive the message of God's grace must learn to do so with grace in our speech. Too commonly, even those who know the gospel well undermine their own words by coming across as pompous or know-it-alls. We harshly confront on minor points and choose hills not worth dying on, or just generally fail to bring a gospel of peace like a peacemaker. Sound remedies to these bad habits are presented here. I hope Gospel Smugness will get a wide reading!"

— DENNIS GUNDERSEN, *Sapulpa Bible Church; author of: Your Child's Profession of Faith and A Praying Church*

"'Truth in love.' It is a high standard, but it is a biblical standard, for our communication. It is never acceptable to take one and leave the other. This is why I so appreciate Blake Long's effort to hold both uncompromisingly within the pages of this book, and to help us all do the same."

— JUSTIN HUFFMAN, *lead pastor of Morningstar in Toronto, and author of the Daily Devotion app*

"Christians increasingly live in a culture antagonistic to our beliefs. The growing sentiment is that Christianity doesn't align with our nation's convictions and dogmas. Simply stated: the gospel, and biblical teachings, offend. The key for us as Christians is to make sure it is the truth of God that is offensive and not ourselves. We need to stand firm in our beliefs, but we don't want to become the cause of offense. In Gospel Smugness, Blake Long helps us work through this challenge, and to see the path forward."

— **ERIK REED**, *Pastor of The Journey Church and,*
  Founder of Knowing Jesus Ministries

"Some of us thrive on controversy while others avoid it at all cost. This book is helpful for both. Blake Long displays compassionate boldness as he directs our hearts to see past simply embracing or avoiding controversy, and into modeling the greatest evangelist of all time: Jesus Christ. Gospel Smugness is a timely call for us to desperately ask God to super naturally reorient our heart to delightful and compassionate evangelism."

—**DILLON CHASE**, *recording artist*

"By example and word, Scripture reminds us repeatedly that it is not our repentance that leads God to be kind to us, but rather it is God's kindness that leads us to repent. Is it any wonder, then, why the most effective method and tone for sharing the good news of Christ is also from a posture of kindness? As it has been said, people will not care how much we know unless and until they know how much we care. Blake has done a wonderful job painting a vision for that kind of engagement in this book. He wisely reminds us that the gospel is itself offensive enough to our sinful, self-justifying sensibilities. Why add to the offense when we could, instead, be warmly welcoming friends, neighbors, and colleagues into the remedy Christ has offered to our offenses?"

—**SCOTT SAULS**, *senior pastor of Christ Presbyterian Church and author of several books, including Jesus Outside the Lines and Beautiful People Don't Just Happen.*

• • •

GOSPEL SMUGNESS

Displaying Christlike Character in Evangelism

• • •

BLAKE LONG

THEOLOGY & LIFE

Applying theology to life

ISBN: 978-0-578-82551-9

First Edition

Cover design: Dustin Benge

Interior design: John Manning

Editor: Meek Manuscripts

Because of the dynamic nature of the Internet, any web addresses or links contained in this book may have changed since publication and may no longer be valid.

To my wife, Shale,

Thank you for your encouragement
and confidence in me.
I am eternally grateful for you.

Contents

...

Foreword

• • •

TRUTHFUL LOVE

"Speaking the truth in love, we are to grow up in every way into him who is the head, into Christ"

Ephesians 4:15

In Ephesians 4, the Apostle Paul points out a logical progression for the church—gifted leaders equip the saints, the saints do the work of ministry, and the body is built up. The results of a built-up body are unity, deep fellowship, Christlikeness, knowledge of sound doctrine, and a dynamic, loving, caring evangelism to the world. Then, Paul reminds us that it is from the Lord Jesus Christ that all of this properly flows. The church is equipped by Christ and grows into Christ so that it may build "itself up in love" (Eph 4:16).

Paul identifies "love" as a notable characteristic of mature believers. That love manifests itself through a Christlike life, mature thinking, and ultimately culminates in a language representing both. That language identifies true believers as those who speak "the truth in love" (Eph. 4:15). Paul forges together love and maturity. If you are mature, you will speak the truth in love. If you do not speak the truth in love, you are not mature.

It's increasingly shocking across social media platforms, and within Christian circles, many professing believers do not speak the truth in love. They brow-beat, slander, ridicule, mock, and treat the truth as nothing more than a club with which to bash their opponents. Such an attitude automatically marks believers, if they are true believers at all, as extremely immature.

During the ministry of Christ, again and again, Peter had to be rebuked because he took the truth into his own hands and often dispensed it in an unloving manner. In the Garden of Gethsemane, for instance, Peter was so zealous for the truth that he took up the sword and aimed for the head of Malchus, cutting off his ear instead (John 18:10). It would be years later, after much maturing in the faith that the same sword-wielding Peter would write, "Above all, keep loving one another earnestly, since love covers a multitude of sins" (1 Pet. 4:8).

Those who are mature in the faith and speak the truth in love will communicate the gospel more effectively. Immature, fractured, fighting Christians have no platform for evangelism and heralding the good news of the gospel and are viewed by the world as the antithesis of what they proclaim. Believers not only speak the truth in love, but they also demonstrate sensitivity and a loving attitude toward everyone. Paul is saying that we are not only to speak the truth in love, but we are to be loving people.

The natural outgrowth of such love expressed in speaking and acting will result in expanding the church. Interestingly, in Acts 2, when the church is described as those who met together for prayer, communion, fellowship, and the apostles' doctrine, it never mentions anything about evangelism. However, Luke tells us, "the Lord added to the church daily" (Acts 2:47). Throughout the book of Acts, we read of the church's tremendous growth as they were equipping the saints and instructing in sound doctrine. The lesson is clear:

evangelism is a by-product of Christian maturity. This was God's pattern when the church was birthed in the first century, and it remains God's pattern today. There is no shortcut or new methodology that will achieve the same lasting success. Ongoing church growth and success comes from following God's prescribed pattern—maturity, sound doctrine, and love.

Ask yourself the next time you are sharing the gospel, "Am I speaking in a loving manner that honors Christ? Am I communicating the gospel in such a way that this individual genuinely thinks that I love them?" This love, ultimately flowing through us from Christ, will always mature believers, build the church, and avoid the smugness that often accompanies immature faith.

DUSTIN BENGE
Provost and professor of church history
Union School of Theology, Wales

Blake Long

Acknowledgments

...

I have so many people to thank in making this book come to fruition. It's been such a journey writing my first book, and I had a massive amount of support along the way from so many people.

First, my fellow church members at Sovereign Grace Bible Church. You all continued to be so excited about the book and always asked questions about when it would come out and what I was writing on. It's been incredible being a part of Sovereign for many years now.

Second, my pastors at Sovereign Grace Bible Church: Randy Tyler, Justin Wright, Paul Wilson, and Paul Priest (Ronnie Qualls as well, even though he is pastoring a different church now). You all have had a tremendous impact on the content of this book. Thank you for your commitment to the gospel of Jesus Christ!

Third, to those who contributed to this book: Dustin Benge, who was kind enough to write the foreword and design the cover, and has become a dear friend. Russell Meek, who cleaned up the rough draft of the manuscript so I would sound less illiterate. John Manning, who did a fantastic job on the interior design of this book. And to those who endorsed it: Dennis Gunderson, Don Currin, Justin Huffman, Justin Peters, Kofi Adu-Boahen, Dillon Chase, Erik Reed—thank you for taking time to read a book by a novice author.

Fourth, to my ever-so-incredible wife, Shale. You are the love of my life. You were by my side the whole way. You sacrificed relaxing nights so I could get this book finished. You were selfless. I thank God every day for you.

Fifth, and most importantly, to my Lord and Savior, Jesus Christ. I am nothing without Christ. This book doesn't happen without His grace and mercy.

Blake Long

...

Preface

...

I didn't plan on writing this. Ever since I began to read vigorously, I knew I wanted to become an author one day. But I didn't plan for this to be the book.

It all began with a blog post that, quite honestly, I threw together in two days. I had the idea in my mind, wrote it, and almost didn't publish it. Next thing I know, Tim Challies shared it on his site—that was the most traffic I've ever seen on my blog. It being shared and receiving that much attention revealed that there was something there. I could expound on this.

The more I thought about it, the more I found other ways to hash out the main point of that blog. Then one day, after much prayer, I committed to writing this book. And the following is the result.

My hope and prayer is that this book blesses and is a means of grace in your walk with Jesus.

Blake Long
February, 2021

...

Introduction

...

The culture would like Christians to know something: they're offended. Being offended has become the new fad in society. It's the liberal's[1] favorite way to virtue signal. It's the zeitgeist of the 21st century. From "safe spaces" at universities to unconstitutional attempts to tear down free speech because of opposing worldviews, being offended is the new "thing."

With that said, why are people getting so offended by what others say? Why do certain segments of the population seem to be in constant uproar? Why does it seem that at every corner Christians are being told to shut up?

It's because of the gospel of Jesus Christ.

---

[1] Since this is the first instance of the word liberal in the book, I should clarify something. In this sentence—and in every other instance of this word—I am not speaking about all who claim to be liberal. Not all liberals are like the ones I speak of in this book. There are many who profess to be liberal that are wonderful people, but just may have different views on controversial issues. I am not speaking about those, but the more "radical" ones.

THE GOSPEL IS OFFENSIVE

Many are quick to be offended by Christians and I understand why. We proclaim a message that, at its core, is offensive to man. It places them under God's condemnation and wrath (John 3:17). The Bible says that man's heart is deceitful above all things (Jeremiah 17:9), and that the very message of the gospel implies that something is horribly wrong with man. Jesus dying on the cross for sinners shows people that they're not what they're supposed to be. You wouldn't think it would come as a surprise, but many people are shocked to hear that the Bible says they are bad people.

Of course, there are other reasons why Christians offend people. For 2,000 plus years Christians have believed in the same historical tenets: the exclusivity of Jesus Christ, the oneness of God, salvation by grace, and much more. Yes, you read that correctly: even the idea of being saved by grace alone offends people. Why is that? It is because people want to contribute. They have so much pride in their hearts that for somebody—the Son of God, no less—to do everything on their behalf is downright insulting. "That implies I can't do it on my own!" they say. They're exactly right.

Moreover, society revolts at the idea of there being only one road to heaven; it infuriates people that Christians believe there is only one God. Christians know this. They embrace the doctrines of Christianity that ignite hatred in the hearts of unbelievers. But it's also strange to unbelievers. Many find Christians to be embarrassing. "In the eyes of the secular world," said Albert Mohler, President of Southern Baptist Theological Seminary, "Christians—and evangelicals in particular—are increasingly an embarrassment."[2] The outside world frowns upon evangelicals because we worship a man who rose from the dead.

---

[2] Albert Mohler, *We Cannot Be Silent: Speaking truth to a culture redefining sex, marriage, & the very reason of right and wrong* (Nashville, TN: Thomas Nelson, 2015), 138.

Every Christian who faithfully follows Jesus will also faithfully look like a clown to the culture. So be it! Let's put on our clown masks and not be ashamed of the gospel (Romans 1:16).

Even still, this raises a question. Why is it strange to unbelievers? We can call it strange, but I think the biblical way of putting it is that "the word of the cross is folly to those who are perishing, but to us who are being saved it is the power of God" (1 Corinthians 1:18). Unbelievers simply don't understand. They see a person dying for sinners and ask, "Why on earth would Jesus do that?" Of course, that is a great question to lead them to the heart of the gospel. Even believers should ask that question. *Why did Jesus do it? Why did the Father send His Son? Why die this gruesome death on behalf of sinners?*

They don't "get it" because they are still in their sin. Satan has blinded their eyes to the beauty of the gospel, the person and work of Jesus Christ (2 Corinthians 4:4). It won't make sense to them until God allows it to make sense. Until then, many unbelievers will see it as hate speech.

WHEN DISAGREEMENT EQUALS HATRED

There's a hilarious episode of *The Office* where an employee, ahem, uses the bathroom in Michael Scott's office. While waiting for it to be cleaned, Michael glances at Stanley (who is African-American) and says: "I am a victim of a hate crime. Stanley knows what I'm talking about." To which Stanley, rather annoyed, retorts: "That's not what a hate crime is." Michael, being the moron he is, responds: "Well, I hated it, a lot, okay."

Now I am not saying liberals are morons, but the same situation is true for individuals who are offended by Christians for simply sharing their faith. Just because they hate what they're hearing doesn't mean it is hate speech. Just because it doesn't sit well with you doesn't mean it's coming from a heart of hate.

The problem resides in that many non-Christians are beginning to equate disagreement with hate. If a Christian disagrees with somebody on LGBTQ issues, for example, they are marked as hateful bigots. Why is that?

Before we have any knee-jerk reactions, let's actually try to understand why others say things like that, albeit untrue.

THEIR IDENTITY

The answer can be summed up with one word: *identity*. We see this all over the news. People despise the Christian worldview—definitely when it comes to sexuality—because to them, it's an attack on their identity, not mere belief. Of course, there's going to be disagreement over what identity exactly means, but that is surely the fundamental reason why Christians are labeled homophobic. When a Christian says homosexuality is wrong, the unbeliever hears, "Who you *are* as a person is wrong." From the unbeliever's perspective, we're attacking the person, not the ideology. Homosexuals (at least most of them) don't look at their homosexuality as a choice but as *who they are*. As a result, they hear hatred when believers say homosexuality is against God's good design.

However, this is part of the problem, right? We must find common ground. We need to help them understand we're not attacking them, but solely their ideas—and we must do so with gentleness and respect (1 Peter 3:15). We believe they're made in the *imago Dei*, the image of God. Christians don't hate unbelievers, we simply disagree—*and that should be okay.*

OTHER ISSUES

This isn't an issue solely with homosexuality, of course. That's just one cultural example among many. Abortion is another one. Many liberals think Christians hate women because we say abortion is murder. They look at it as an attack on women's "reproductive rights," which is a preposterous euphemism for . . . the procedure that kills babies. (You don't have the "right" to do that!) And with all issues—sexuality, abortion, gender—many liberals incessantly call us intolerant.

How ironic.

THE NEW TOLERANCE

Liberals champion "tolerance." It's the golden rule of liberalism, so to speak. They believe conservatives—Christians in particular—are intolerant because of the Christian worldview. However, the ideological elephant in the room is that countless people have redefined the word *tolerance*. They have twisted it around to mean *acceptance* or *approval*. If you don't approve—no, even celebrate—their views, you are an intolerant imbecile. This is not extreme. This is quickly becoming the center of liberalism.

In today's world, if you dare give a different view on a hot-button topic, you're not simply disagreeing with them—you're being intolerant.[3] Yet the irony is that this is when true intolerance comes bursting forward. In the name of leftist "tolerance," they are intolerant. To many, it's either approve or shut up. No middle ground.

With that being said, what exactly is this buzzword tolerance? Tolerance is simply the art of accepting that different ideas exist. You can talk to somebody—whether it's a normal conversation about religion, politics, etc.—and not have them rip your head off because of your views. Tolerance is a beautiful thing when correctly exercised. We should be able to love each other while disagreeing. Love and disagreement

---

[3] Like I said in an earlier footnote, there are certainly exceptions to this but it is beginning to look like a normal reaction.

shouldn't be viewed as mutually exclusive; you can genuinely do both.

I don't have to agree with you to love you. I love you regardless because you're a fellow image bearer of God. And that even goes for other Christians with whom I disagree. We are both people; we both have the same value, worth, and dignity because God has given it to us. As a result, we should be able to disagree even on a fundamental worldview issue.

THE GOSPEL AND OFFENSIVENESS

By now, you may be asking what this book is even about. Parts of this introduction were fairly negative toward many who hold different views than Christians. My goal in that was not to demonize but to reveal we are living in a time of inconsistency. Christians have to navigate new things every day. And with that, we have to navigate sharing the gospel to them.

Sometimes I think Christians have a problem. We may have the right message and say the right things, but too many times we negate the truth with how we behave. In other words, we add to the offensive nature of the gospel by being jerks—flat out obnoxious.

The central theme of this book is this: how to biblically communicate an offensive gospel with discretion while simultaneously keeping the message intact. In other words: sharing an offensive gospel with an offended culture, while displaying Christlike character.

In light of all that has been said so far, ask yourself this question: How do we share the gospel while not being offensive in the process, given the toxic culture you just read about? Before we answer that question, let's talk about some of the general ways that we fail in this area, and then get into specifics.

•••

{ 1 }

...

The Gospel is Offensive Enough

...

A couple of years ago there was a man that came to the local university in my town to open-air preach. This was no Ray Comfort-type street preacher. What he did was nothing akin to biblical preaching. Rather than hear Christ and Him crucified (1 Corinthians 2:2), all that was heard was fearmongering and hate. Instead of hearing the good news of the gospel, onlookers heard something similar to the bad news of the infamous Westboro Baptist Church.

It was a message of morality without Jesus. Dos and don'ts without redemption. Begrudging obedience without hope. He correctly condemned fornication, homosexuality, and other sins. But that was the end of the message. No Jesus, no cross, no resurrection, no forgiveness, no hope—only condemnation.

What this man misunderstood is that the world is already condemned (John 3:17). The world needs the light of the gospel, not more condemnation. And not only was the message off but his tone was too. Yelling through a megaphone, he came across as superior, as if he had all knowledge and was shoving it in their faces.

To put it plainly: he was an obnoxious jerk. He resembled the people the apostle Paul described as "having a zeal for God, but not according to knowledge" (Romans 10:1-3).

It may not be to this extent, but we can be this way too even if we preach the right message. Instead of letting the gospel offend, we ourselves do the offending by how we speak and interact with others.

WHEN YOU'RE JUST BEING A JERK

As Bible-believing Christians, we must ardently stand behind the fact that the gospel will offend. These are dire times, so we should not cower in fear. Now is not the time to duck from the chaos but to step into it—with the gospel! With that said, we frequently fall into the sinful trap of being offensive ourselves. "So the gospel itself is already offensive enough," Trip Lee said in an interview at *Desiring God*. "We don't need to add offense to it by being jerks about everything. We don't need to add offense to it by being very condemning and self-righteous. We don't need to add offense to it by being incapable of actually loving and being in relationship with people. We really want to show people the compassion of Jesus even as we say very hard things."[4]

We don't want to be people who are "incapable of actually loving and being in relationship with people." We want to show the love of Jesus through sharing the gospel, but our sin gets in the way. Our pride, ego, and sarcasm get in the way. This happens because we take our eyes off of who we used to be.

REGAINING EMPATHY

We use to be the other person (1 Corinthians 6:9-11). It was once us who got offended by the hard message of the gospel.

---

[4] Trip Lee, "Don't Be a Jerk When the World Doesn't Like You," *Desiring God*, May 19, 2015, https://www.desiringgod.org/interviews/dont-be-a-jerk-when-the-world-doesnt-like-you.

We were the ones who had our minds blinded by the god of this world, Satan (2 Corinthians 4:4). We lose sight of the fact that it was God who brought us out of the muck and mire of our sin, not ourselves. But God (Ephesians 2:4), not but *Blake*.

It is easier to treat others poorly when we forget that our salvation wasn't achieved by us. But when we remember the *but God*, we remember that nobody is beyond redemption. As a result, we are reminded to have empathy for others. We are reminded to care for others like we care for ourselves. We are reminded of the importance of walking in someone else's shoes. Practicing empathy goes a long way in an evangelistic encounter.

WE'RE TALKING TO SOULS

And then there is the problem of treating people as mere numbers, not souls. We have good motives, but good motives only go so far. The temptation to be a jerk still resides in a heart of good motivation. We may share the gospel well but we forget we're talking to another human.

When we look at them as a mere number, we are prone to not care as much about the person. It becomes customary to focus more on gaining another number for God's Kingdom instead of simply having a conversation with another image-bearer of God.

In short, we forget the *imago Dei*.

FORGETTING THE IMAGO DEI

Every person is made in the image of God (Genesis 1:27). They have just as much value, dignity, and worth as the next man because we've all been fearfully and wonderfully made by God (Psalm 139:14). God knit each of us together in our mother's womb (Psalm 139:13).

With that in the forefront of our minds, we begin to act more like Jesus in our witness. In remembering the *imago Dei*, it becomes easier to talk to all types of people with the love of Jesus, instead of the love of Blake. Remembering that all people are made in God's image plays a huge role in how we treat people. It doesn't matter who you're speaking with—you need to treat them like another human being. It doesn't matter how fierce the disagreement is. We have the responsibility as God's ambassadors on earth to treat all people with love and respect—even in the midst of a tense gospel conversation.

THREE GODLY TRAITS

The apostle Paul was known for his unwavering commitment to truth, whether it be about God's sovereign choice in Romans 9 or confronting Peter in Galatians 2 (which I will get to later). In Galatians 5:22-23 Paul strikes us right in our sinful hearts: *"But the fruit of the Spirit is love, joy, peace, patience, kindness, goodness, faithfulness, gentleness, self-control; against such things there is no law."* These characteristics must be consistently shown in the people of God. I don't intend to cover each of these characteristics, but I do want to talk about three of them as it pertains to displaying Christlike character in evangelism: kindness, gentleness, and self-control.

Are you a kind Christian? Followers of Jesus should be the kindest people. I know we know what kindness means, but practically speaking, what does it look like? I am afraid that sometimes we need to refresh our memory as kindness escapes even the most mature Christians.

True kindness is Spirit-produced; that is, it is supernatural. It is a generous orientation of our hearts toward people regardless of whether they deserve it. We see this supernatural kindness in God, whose kindness is meant to lead us to repentance (Romans 2:4). Our supreme goal as Christians is to imitate Christ, the "exact imprint of his [God's] nature"

(Hebrews 1:3). Therefore, we should see that Christ was the kindest of all and strive to be like Him. Knowing that God has saved us by His grace in Christ (Ephesians 2:8-9), this marvelous salvation should propel us forward to be kind Christians.

Practically, kindness means not reacting to a snide comment but instead responding with kindness, even if it means the other person "wins" the argument. Remember, we're not looking to win arguments; we're looking to win people to Jesus. Argumentation doesn't lead anybody to see the beauty of Jesus.

Additionally, being kind means swallowing our pride and not succumbing to the temptation of having the last word. Do you have a sibling? If so, then you know this from firsthand experience. Every time you two argued, it was your mission to have the last word—and your sibling felt the same way. Having the last word gave you a sense of pride and one-upsmanship. Eventually, you start arguing about who will have the last word instead of what you were arguing about originally.

With Jesus, however, there is no arguing. Jesus, the divine Son of God—the Beginning and the End—will have the last word whether you get the last word or not. This fruit of the Spirit is immensely underrated. We need to be kind people. So, believer . . . are you kind to others?

Are you a gentle Christian? Next to kindness is gentleness, another undervalued fruit of the Spirit. Gentleness is lacking in many Christians today, including myself. We are all guilty of it.

Being gentle doesn't mean be cowardly or timid in evangelism. Not in the slightest. It does, however, mean not reacting explosively to disagreement. It means letting insults go in one ear and out the other. It means we should bleed mercy. When pricked, grace and mercy must spill out—that is gentleness.

God calls us to be people who overflow with mercy and grace just as He overflows with mercy and grace *for us*. Are you a gentle person or do you struggle with showing grace to people? For example, sometimes being gentle means holding your tongue when all you want to do is argue (remember our talk about not needing to get the last word?). Think about it; examine your heart and ask God if you're gentle. God will not turn away a plea for more gentleness, my friend. He answers the prayers of His children pleading to be more like His Son.

With that being said, both of these characteristics—kindness and gentleness—won't be consistent within us if we do not have self-control.

Are you a self-controlled Christian? If we want to display kindness and gentleness—or any other Christlike characteristic for that matter—we must first have self-control. In his book *Your Future Self Will Thank You: Secrets to Self-Control from the Bible and Brain Science (A Guide for Sinners, Quitters, and Procrastinators)*, Drew Dyck brings home this same point: "Think about it. Can you be faithful to your spouse without self-control? Can you be generous without self-control? Peaceable? Selfless? Honest? Kind? No, even the most basic altruism requires suspending your own interests to think of others."[6]

You can't be a kind or gentle Christian without first being a self-controlled Christian. If you don't have self-control, it's more difficult to contain your sin, thereby making kindness and gentleness virtually absent from your life. And we must understand self-control is not some type of awful restriction. Self-control is not a straight jacket. "The Bible portrays self-control not as restrictive but rather as the path to freedom," Dyck explained. "It enables us to do what's right—and ultimately what is best for us."[7]

---

[6] Drew Dyck, *Your Future Self Will Thank You: Secrets to Self-Control from the Bible and Brain Science (A Guide for Sinners, Quitters, and Procrastinators)* (Chicago: Moody Publisher, 2019, 17.
[7] Ibid, 19

Self-control frees us to be who we are supposed to be like: Jesus. But doing that is hard. Possessing self-control is a fruit of the Spirit we talk about a lot but struggle to display. It's tough—no ifs, ands, or buts about it. However, just because exercising self-control is tough doesn't mean we should neglect to pursue it. I can't tell you how many times I wanted to quit playing golf in my formative years because . . . it was just too hard. That's not the right attitude to have. You don't quit because things are hard. Rather, it should make you try harder.

In the same vein with self-control, we shouldn't stop striving to have it just because it's difficult to display. All it means is we need to rely more on Jesus to display it.

Getting more practical, do you have enough self-control to not blurt out the first thing that comes to mind? I'm sure we can all admit the first thing that comes to mind is, for the most part, never helpful, gracious, or loving. When snide remarks are the natural response, we need the Spirit to help us respond in a supernatural way. We desperately need His help, because it's unfortunately too normal for us to be jerks when we talk with people. Do you want to know the fast track to not being offensive? Have self-control.

There are more than three fruits of the Spirit but these three are enough to make us humble. We have to pull in the reigns of our smugness when witnessing because our sin is sneaky. We must work (from Christ's work) to be Christians who, when stabbed, bleed out kindness, gentleness, and self-control.

MAKING OTHERS FEEL DUMB

On occasion we tend to make others feel unintelligent. We might explain the concept of grace and they simply don't understand. Our natural inclination at that point is to say, "How does that not make sense? Grace is something that is given to us that we don't deserve." But did we ever think about the fact that this specific person might've grown up in a legalistic background, where grace was distorted?

It's of utmost importance for us to be gracious in explaining things to others who have a hard time understanding. Everybody is different. We have to be intentional about how we make others feel in gospel conversations. Feelings aren't everything, of course. Yes, facts are more important than feelings—but feelings still matter. The last thing we want to do is make somebody seem stupid. Even more than this is the problem of when we claim to love someone, but say something in a manner that quite frankly shows we do not love him or her.

LET YOUR LOVE BE GENUINE

Some Christians will say, "I tell you this because I love you," but they are conveying the message in a condescending, I'm-better-than-you fashion. We are not better than anybody else; we've simply been redeemed by the blood of Jesus.

It doesn't matter if we preface our point with "I say this because I love you"—you might be saying the right thing but in the wrong way. And when you do that, you lose the message. In simply echoing a phrase but not meaning it, you show yourself to be insensitive.

Showing love is not simply sharing the gospel but sharing the gospel with a *gracious, compassionate tone.* If we share the gospel but do so in an abrasive, blunt manner—what good has been done? Yes, we got to the gospel (Philippians 1:15-18) but did so in a not-so-loving manner, which makes things difficult. People are not prone to believe the gospel when it comes from an attitude of superiority. The good news may have been proclaimed, but did the tone in your voice cover it up?

ATTITUDE ADJUSTMENTS FOR THE GOSPEL

We will continue to have times when we fail, but we should be sensitive to the potential ways we could be offensive in our witness. It's important to understand that our witness is not merely in strict evangelism. I'm not just talking about street preaching or having a formal gospel conversation with someone. Our witness has to do with what the watching world sees. Our public witness makes a difference in how unbelievers perceive Christianity. There is much nuance there, but we must do our part in making sure our witness to the gospel is faithful.

If we don't have a faithful witness, drastic steps may need to be taken. This is why being part of a local church is important. If you consistently struggle in this area, confess that to your pastor and/or other church members and be open to accountability. You will not grow as a Christian—definitely in evangelism—if you do not have other like-minded Christians holding you accountable.

Are you making a habit of being an obnoxious know-it-all and argument starter? Do you just love causing kerfuffles? When tensions rise, what is your go-to move? Maybe it's time for you to self-reflect and see why you act this way. The gospel transcends our egos.

Friends, we need to do much repenting—the gospel is worth it. We need to see our sin in order to see His beauty. We need to admit our tendency to be offensive so we may not be a hindrance to the gospel's message.

Yes, the gospel is offensive, and we must be fine with that. We must stand behind that. But we must not add to its offensiveness. Let the gospel do the offending—not you. And this begins at the foundational level of guarding our mouths.

•••

{ 2 }

...

Guarding Our Mouths

...

The tongue is a very small member of your body. It is also the most ferocious. The tongue, as James says, is like one tiny spark that starts a forest fire (James 3:5-6). Though it may be tiny, it has the power to destroy. It also has the power to build up.

How we use our tongues determine how effective we are in our witness; and not only our witness, but also all spheres of life. The words we speak give evidence to the spiritual maturity of our hearts. Are you consistently ensuring that you think before you speak? Are you being vigilant about being slow to speak (James 1:19)?

Like I said at the end of the previous chapter, the majority of ensuring we aren't offensive in gospel conversations is discerning when to speak up or be quiet. Very often our quick mouth is the reason people leave the conversation more opposed to the gospel than before. Our mouths get us into trouble.

CHRISTIANS ARE SUPPOSED TO BE DIFFERENT

We live in a culture that, for the most part, does not care about taming its tongue. Whether it is politics, religion, or some strange animal in between, society at large has no regard for closing its mouth. If people have something to say—whether smart or not, kind or not, false or not—they are going to say it because it makes them feel better. The prevailing culture doesn't really live by the "if you don't have something nice to say, don't say it" rule of kindness anymore.

Instead, what we see around our society is vitriol, hate, and intolerance that spew from mouths like somebody doing a spit take. To be fair, there are many unbelievers who are very nice people with whom Christians will disagree. That's not a debate and this isn't directed toward them. I am pointing my finger at the more hateful side of society that say, "It's either my way or the highway, and if you don't agree, I will make sure you're 'canceled.'"

Christians aren't surprised to see this. This type of behavior that doesn't bridle the tongue is rooted in a deep hatred and disdain for their Creator. Scripture tells us this. What I am concerned about is that Christians are doing the same thing. We are not so quick to guard our tongues, but rather are quick to speak and fast to get agitated. We may love the Lord but many times our speech doesn't show it.

PRESERVE OR RUIN YOUR LIFE

The book of Proverbs is filled with sayings about how important the mouth is. One of my favorite verses on this subject resides in Proverbs 13:3, which says: "Whoever guards his mouth preserves his life; he who opens wide his lips come to ruin."

What a counter-cultural statement. If you guard your mouth, you'll preserve your life. If you don't, your life will be in shambles. This isn't necessarily saying if you keep yapping your mouth it will kill you one day—although I am sure that could happen if you were talking too much to the wrong person. This speaks more to the fact of one's reputation. If you guard your mouth, your reputation will precede you. If you open your mouth too much, there won't be much of a reputation there.

And I fear that, for many Christians, they have a reputation—it is simply a bad one. They've gained this bad reputation because they have a hard time keeping their mouth closed. Whether they simply like to hear themselves talk or enjoy arguing too much, it becomes a problem when you're known for the rude things you say. Do you want to be a Christian who has a bad case of word vomit?

I don't pretend to be the guru here. All Christians will struggle from time to time with knowing when to stop talking. But my focus here is more on Christians who make a habit out of opening their mouth too frequently. Their tongue is not tamed. They aren't intentional about letting others speak. They become so focused on what they have to say that not only are they not taming their tongue—they are also not listening. Their mouths are not preserving their lives but making it come to ruin. In short, their words are careless.

EVERY CARELESS WORD

Many Christians have a difficult time holding their tongue. Whether you have a hard time not talking over people or you habitually say things that are inappropriate or rude, we all need to take heed of the words from Jesus in Matthew 12:36-37. We should perpetually remind ourselves that Jesus will make us account for every careless word we speak.

In other words, we need wisdom—wisdom from above. Wisdom from the Holy Spirit that lives inside us. Most of the time the reason we are careless with our words is not because we have malicious intent to verbally hurt somebody but because we don't have much wisdom in how to speak to others. In short, many Christians are immature. So, what should we do?

We should do the best thing we can always do: look to Jesus Christ.

WHEN JESUS SPOKE UP

One early morning Jesus went to the temple. When He did, everybody came up to Him and He started to teach. As this happened, the scribes and Pharisees brought a woman to him who had been caught in adultery. The teachers of the law asked Him what they should do with her; they were trying to stump Jesus with another "gotcha" question. But Jesus wasn't having it. He bent down and wrote something in the sand (who knows what He wrote). Once He stood back up, He said the popular statement the whole world espouses: "Let him who is without sin among you be the first to throw a stone at her" (John 8:7).

In this response Jesus was pointing out their awful hypocrisy. They bring this woman to Jesus and it wasn't even about her. It was about them trying to corner Jesus. They wanted to catch Him off guard. I guess they didn't know it's impossible to catch the Son of God off guard. By now, you'd think they had learned their lesson not to do that. For a moment Jesus didn't saying anything as He wrote in the sand, but then He said those words that are repeated even by the vilest of sinners to excuse their sin.

In this instance it was appropriate for Him to speak up. He was not only answering the Pharisees' question in His own God-in-the-flesh way, but He was also proclaiming a message of hope, of forgiveness, of redemption. He was sharing a message with a vulnerable woman that would give light to her life in the midst of darkness, embarrassment, and shame—even if it was shame from her own sin.

After He said that, the teachers walked away and there sat the woman. Jesus spoke to her again and said: "Woman, where are they? Has no one condemned you? She said, 'No one, Lord.' And Jesus said, 'Neither do I condemn you; go, and from now sin no more'" (vv. 10-11).[7]

---

[7] This passage is not in the earlier manuscripts, so there's the possibility this wasn't actually penned by John. Of course, the passage aligns with other teachings of Christ, but it's still possible it's not something that actually happened.

This is one of many passages that give us a good example of when Jesus decided it was time to speak up. Jesus was not only exposing the Pharisees' hypocrisy but also assured this adulteress woman of the redemption found in Him. Jesus, being the Son of God, knows exactly when to speak up. He knows when to confront, when to respond, and when to make a point. Now let's turn to when Jesus decided to remain silent.

THE SILENCE SAID EVERYTHING

As Jesus stood before Pontius Pilate, being heckled by the crowds, He was focused on His mission. Pilate asked Him, "Are you the king of the Jews?" and Jesus answered, "You have said so" (Matthew 27:12). Then the text says this: "But when he was accused by the chief priests and elders, he gave no answer. Then Pilate said to him, 'Do you not hear how many things they testify against you?' But he gave him no answer, not even to a single charge, so that the governor was greatly amazed" (vv. 12-14).

Jesus remained silent because His accusers didn't deserve the time of day. From the very beginning of His ministry He was falsely accused because the things He said infuriated the religious leaders of the day. It angered them because left and right He would bring to light their hypocrisy. As He stood before Pilate with charges brought against Him, He didn't *need* to respond. They didn't deserve a response. His life spoke for itself. And this "greatly amazed" Pilate. Pilate was amazed that Jesus could stand there silent while all these charges were thrown at Him.

WHAT WOULD YOU DO?

What is your gut reaction when you are falsely accused of something? Do you remain silent or do you attempt to defend yourself? Do you keep quiet or lash out in anger because your name is being tossed through the mud?

Because Jesus is sinless (Hebrews 4:15), we can't fully put ourselves in His shoes because we deal with sin every day. However, I am sure we've all faced false allegations in our lifetime. The question for you, Christian, is this: how do you respond?

With anything in life, I think it's wise to follow the example of Jesus in this circumstance. The first inclination is to defend ourselves. We crave having a good reputation. We want this! We want to be above reproach; we want people to respect us and have no ill will toward us. But that's simply not the reality for all people. Because you follow Jesus, the world will hate you (John 15:18). We know and embrace this. Since the world hates us, there will be times when we are falsely accused. There will be times people say hurtful things about us they know aren't true—but they do it anyway because it causes Christians to look bad. Take comfort, Christian: even when you're made to look bad, remember that Jesus is still good. And we're the ones who have Jesus.

And remember, many times your response is what the accuser is looking for. They want you to get worked up; they want you to cause a scene even when you're the victim. It feeds their immaturity.

In the majority of these circumstances, the most Christlike thing you can do happens to be the least natural. And what is that? *Don't respond!* Have you done something wrong? Have you sinned in a particular fashion as to warrant the accusation? If so, confess your sin(s), repent, and move on. But if you have not done anything wrong, stay silent, even when it goes against every fiber of your being.

Christian, please understand this: you don't need to respond. You are a justified child of God. You have been purchased, bought by the blood of the Lamb. Who can bring a charge against God's elect (Romans 8:33)? Nobody. You have nothing to prove. Trust in Jesus and ignore the allegations.

With that being said, we have a difficult time ignoring false accusations because we're sinners. Though we're justified in the eyes of God, we have that nagging sense of self-justification. We want to clear our name. In most occasions we decided to speak up. Of course, there's nothing inherently wrong with responding. Gently respond if you're able to do so. If you respond with gospel-mindedness, by all means—respond! Hit 'em with the gospel.

Unfortunately, our sin-saturated hearts don't let us do that. Instead of calm responses to accusations—or no response—we quickly retort with fierce defensiveness. The desire to defend our name is good. That's not the issue. The issue arises when we are so vehement to the point that it would be better to keep our mouths closed. "Well, you did this!" or "You did that!" we say. In our attempt to defend our reputation, we become one in the same with the accuser.

Here's my point: we need to be aware of our emotions and natural inclinations. How do you usually respond to confrontation or accusations? Do you have a bad temper or can you keep yourself from getting too upset? Do you respond with gentleness and a call to repent in a loving manner? Or do you allow your righteous anger to take hold of you, transform into sinful anger, and lash out in tears?

Think about it. Be aware of your own shortcomings. If you believe you won't respond well, then ignore. If you think you will respond with gentleness, then it's probably fine for you to respond. It simply takes discernment. If you don't know how you'd respond, ask your pastors or people close to you what the best course of action is. And before you do anything else, pray!

With all that said, in most cases, the best thing for you to do is ignore the accusation. Be like Jesus: respond when a response is warranted. If there's no benefit for you to respond, then don't reply. Sometimes a reply opens up the floodgates into a long, drawn-out argument. Don't take the bait.

WHAT ABOUT WHEN WE WITNESS?

Of course, the whole point of this book is centered on our witness in evangelism. In light of that, ponder this question: if you are accused of something in a witnessing conversation, what do you do? The answer depends a lot on the question and the attitude of the person accusing.

If the person you're speaking with is friendly and personable, but accuses you of something, it would be wise to respond. If the conversation is cordial then responding to an accusation won't be too big of a deal. Just take care to make sure the conversation doesn't go chasing any squirrels.

For instance, if the person says, "Christians are so narrow-minded to believe their religion is the only correct one." This is a typical accusation brought against Christians. If I put myself in the unbeliever's shoes (having empathy for others!), I can understand the accusation, but it ultimately falls short. In this scenario, it would be wise of you to kindly respond to this with the intention of pushing the conversation more toward the gospel. There's no point to go around in circles about whether Christian's are narrow-minded. Convincing somebody that we're not is not going to save them—the gospel is.

Other times, Christians experience false accusations in the midst of a heated conversation with an unbeliever. What should you do? If the accusation is so outrageous then you should probably ignore it. You should quickly change the subject. Say something like, "That's not important to what we're talking about," and then bring up something else that is more relevant to the conversation. However, that's likely easier said than done. Follow the Spirit's guide.

If you are a natural debater—and it's therefore difficult to guard your mouth sometimes—you have to be aware that changing the subject isn't simply for the sake of the conversation but for your sake as well. How many times have Christians made a fool of themselves simply because they were responding to a silly accusation that didn't deserve a response? Just look at social media. The trolls lurk everywhere. They are always there to cause a needless ruckus. Ignore them.

FITLY SPOKEN WORDS

As I mentioned before, the Bible is very clear on how we are to speak and not speak. Our mouth can get us in trouble (Proverbs 21:23), even when we are being falsely accused; it can also encourage and gladden the heart of an anxious person (Proverbs 12:25).

In the context of evangelism, the words we use—and the tone we have—matters greatly. It doesn't matter if you're speaking to an unbeliever—they still need words that are saturated with grace. This doesn't mean avoid talking about the law and sin; it doesn't mean compromise the gospel message. It doesn't even mean not calling them to repentance and faith. It simply means to be intentional about using words that can even encourage or push them in the right direction.

If you're faithful in your witness, you will use words like *sin, hell,* and *wrath.* No unbeliever enjoys those words. But make sure you also say the words *redemption, salvation, forgiveness,* and *eternal life.* Encourage the unbeliever. It's possible to do that. Use words that are "fitly spoken" (Proverbs 25:11-12). Not all unbelievers are antagonistic to the gospel; not all unbelievers are set in their way and want nothing to do with God. There are many unbelievers out there who think about God but merely have wrong assumptions about how Christianity works. Not that these people are truly seeking the Lord, as we know no unbeliever truly seeks the Lord (Romans 3:10-12), but these people are more prone to believe in the gospel when having a conversation with a Christian. They are on the edge and simply haven't pulled the trigger.

Sometimes the words you say in a gospel conversation can be the very thing that propels an unbeliever to profess faith in Christ. Whether it's a clarifying answer to a difficult question or simply your graciousness towards them, anything can happen. God is powerful enough to simply use a Christian's gentleness to propel an unbeliever to repentance and faith (by hearing the gospel, still, of course).

LIFE AND DEATH IN THE TONGUE

"Death and life are in the power of the tongue," Proverbs 18:22 says. This is unequivocally true. Our speech matters. Guarding our mouth matters. The words that come out of our mouths hold within them the power to encourage or anger; to make glad or upset; to compliment or critique. In our witness—and simply in our lives as Christians—we need to be vigilant about what comes forth from our tongues. Since the Holy Spirit has "caused us to be born again" (1 Peter 1:3), our tongues should give evidence to that new life. Our speech should be different than unbelievers. Our words should be gracious and filled with edification, not rudeness or snark. There may be a time and place for light-hearted sarcasm, but most of the time we use it at the wrong time.

Believers, guard your mouths. Know when to speak up; know when to stay quiet. Lean on the power of the Holy Spirit to discern what to do in your situation. Much of guarding your mouth boils down to yielding to the Holy Spirit and not to your flesh. And this applies now more than ever to our presence on social media.

•••

{ 3 }

...

The Christian's Witness on Social Media

...

Social media is wonderful. I have Facebook, Twitter, and Instagram accounts and thoroughly enjoy those mediums. It is a fantastic tool to stay connected with others and also connect with new, like-minded Christians. Social media, though, has an Achilles heel. Due to it's enticing nature, people practically live on social media. The Big Tech companies have succeeded. They know what they're doing. We are on it 24/7 because we want to be *in the know*. We are horrified of not knowing about something. Consequently, social media has sucked us into the vortex of the digital world and we have not gotten out—*and do we even want out?*

Just with other types of technology, social media has blessings and curses. If you don't understand that, you'll be quick to fall into the trap of using it for sinful purposes. Social media is not inherently bad, but exposes man's inherent evil. Therefore, we need to be intentional with how we use social media, and definitely so as it pertains to our witness online.

HAVE A PLAN

As silly as it sounds, Christians need to plan how they use social media. And when I say plan, I don't mean you have to stick to it down to the last iota. My point is that we need to know why we use social media. One of the pitfalls we fall into is constantly being on social media, which leaves us vulnerable to going to places we shouldn't, neglecting other responsibilities, and engaging in vain arguments.

All the more reason to be intentional. Everybody's plan is going to look different—and that is okay. Use social media as a mission field the best way you can.

For example, I only try to use social media to post new blogs, random thoughts, or family things. Outside of that, I do scroll through my feeds, but I try to limit that. Of course, I fail miserably, but I still have the intention in mind.

And without intentionally, you will be victim to mindless scrolling and social media will dictate your life. I am constantly failing at this, so I am not suggesting we can do this perfectly. Just like with everything else in life, we should be intentional about how we conduct ourselves on social media. Are you getting this? Be intentional; be intentional; be intentional.

Run your social media; don't let it run you.

With that said, let's talk a little about ways in which we damage our witness online and how to remedy that.

AVOID VAIN ARGUMENTS

Believers tend to argue about *everything* on social media. From theology to politics to whether *Die Hard* is a Christmas movie or not, the pointless debates never cease. Are there times when arguments are beneficial? Sure, but they are few and far between. I would say use great caution. If you really feel the urge to discuss something with somebody, simply send him or her a private message. Better yet, ask them to meet you for a cup of coffee. When you comment on the public thread, be careful about responding too quickly and with the first thing that comes to mind. Just like we should guard our mouths, we should also guard our typing.

We should remind ourselves that God will hold us accountable for every careless word we type (Matthew 12:36). We saw how serious that was in the last chapter. I believe the command in Matthew 12:36 has been broken millions of times in social media arguments.

Whether it's a one-hundred-comment Facebook thread or the anonymous Twitter troll, the temptation to step into the social media debate perpetually lurks around the corner. To our detriment, we succumb to that temptation—again and again. Facebook and Twitter debates aren't inherently wrong to engage in, of course. The issue is not that social media arguments are innately sinful; the issue is these arguments bring out the worst in God's people. And in turn we do a disservice God's gospel.

WHAT WE SHOULD BE KNOWN FOR

Christians on social media should be known more for what they are *for* rather than what they are *against*. Most of what I see on social media is another Christian describing why he or she is against something, whether it is a particular view on a theological doctrine, the newest heretical video, or if the Southern Baptist Convention is sliding into liberalism (hint: it's not). Though there is much on social media that consists of encouragement and other beneficial material, it seems like the over-critical culture we claim to not be a part of has invaded our social media feeds. We pride ourselves in being "in the world, but not of the world," however, I am not too sure we're following that faithfully on social media.

Believer, we need less criticism and more encouragement; less argumentation and more cordiality. Always barking about what we're against doesn't really do any good. Let's be better for the sake of the gospel. Let's aim to edify instead of criticize.

FORGETTING WHO YOU'RE TALKING TO

It's evident that Christians are guilty of offensive behavior on social media. One of the biggest reasons for that is because we're all behind keyboards (or smartphones). We detach ourselves from the reality that we're still having a conversation with another human being. "A simple rule of thumb to ask yourself before posting: would I say this to the face of the person I am speaking about?" said Read Mercer Schuchardt, associate professor of communication at Wheaton College. "If the answer is no, then edit until the answer is yes. Imagine creating a world in which they actually knew we were Christians by our tweets?"[8] Christ's name is trampled on too many times from tweets that should've stayed in the draft file.

There are many things we say behind our phones or computers that we wouldn't say in person over a drink. That shouldn't be. If you don't have anything constructive to say, you probably shouldn't comment back. Much of the time we ignore this advice because we're so caught up in the debacle. We fight fire with fire; we shoot from the hip and don't flinch. We're taking no prisoners and pulling no punches. In short, we're offensive—and we don't even know it.

Friends, before you get into a big debate on social media, ask yourself if you know the person. If so, then maybe discuss it privately or somewhere else. Too many times we argue with people we don't know and tend to assume the worst motives—and Christians should not be people who assume the worst motives in others.

Why do we fall into this sinful pattern? What makes us act this way on social media? For starters, we think we have to reply to somebody's post or comment.

[8] Read Mercer Schuchardt, "8 Theses on Christians and Twitter," *Crossway*, March 21, 2018, https://www.crossway.org/articles/8-theses-on-christians-and-twitter/.

YOU DON'T HAVE TO RESPOND

You have an unbelieving friend, Johnny. Johnny is a known atheist who in his spare time enjoys mocking the Christian faith. One day, Johnny posts a status on Facebook that is clearly a cry for attention. He posts: "God is just as much real as the tooth fairy. You might as well believe in the Flying Spaghetti Monster."

You've been friends with Johnny since junior high, so you know his personality like nobody else. You know this guy is just bored. In short, you know you probably shouldn't give it the time of day. But the apologetics-loving part of you couldn't resist. You reply—the rest is history. After an hours-long debate over the existence of God, you finally give up after realizing that Johnny's goal has been accomplished: he got you to take the atheist-bait and you wound up looking like a fool on Facebook. (Don't get me wrong, it's certainly possible to have a respectful conversation with a skeptic on social media that is fruitful, but that is rare.)

This happened all because you thought you had to respond to his post. Christian, please hear me: you don't have to respond. Just keep scrolling. You don't have to give it the time of day, definitely when you know the person loves to stir the pot and it brings out your bad side.

What's worse than giving into temptation to respond to somebody stirring the pot? Being the one who is stirring.

STIRRING THE POT

Have you ever written a post on Facebook or tweeted something you knew was going to be controversial? I think the answer is assuredly yes. The answer might be yes for all of us. The better question to ask, though, is do we ever check our hearts before we post or tweet it? Do we examine our motives? Are we posting to plant our feet in the ground of the gospel or are we trying to cause a stir?

It's easy to joke about stirring the pot, but let's face it: stirring the pot is not a fruit of the Spirit. Stirring the theological pot also stirs up division and strife. And we don't want to be people who cause strife, do we (Proverbs 20:3)? The Bible certainly doesn't paint a pretty picture.

But let me rewind a second, here. When I say, "stirring the pot," I don't mean *not* posting something that is going to turn some heads. I have posted many things that will cause believers and unbelievers alike to get angry and comment. That's not wrong. Honestly, it comes down to knowing your own heart. Knowing something you post is going to cause many negative reactions isn't bad. It is only sinful if you are posting it to simply stir the pot or get into heated debates. You shouldn't *want* to debate people on social media. You shouldn't want to post something merely to cause controversy.

Why should you not want to debate people on social media? Because it can reveal that you're a quarrelsome person.[9] Nobody wants to be a quarrelsome person. However, there are some people that take pleasure in getting into quarrels. It fuels them. That's not good. In doing this, we forget something: the whole world is watching.

LETTING THE WHOLE WORLD SEE

When we post something and somebody comments with a question—what do you do? First, you should pray. Pray for wisdom in how you should respond. Remember, there is nothing too small to pray for. God is glorified when you ask for His wisdom in how to respond. It reveals you care about how you come across. You care about God's glory.

---

[9] Kevin DeYoung, "Distinguishing Marks of a Quarrelsome Person," The Gospel Coalition, June 13, 2009, https://www.thegospelcoalition.org/blogs/kevin-deyoung/distinguishing-marks-quarrelsome-person/.

There's something else to take into account: the whole world of Facebook or Twitter can see what's happening—so tread lightly. One of the ways we become an ineffective witness to the gospel is that the people reading the Facebook debate or Twitter exchange see how we're speaking to the other person. They see condescension, arrogance, and holier-than-thou-ism; they don't see love, compassion, and empathy. They see motives assumed; they don't see the benefit of the doubt given. Maybe that's solely their perception . . . or maybe you're actually being offensive. That is something we should ponder.

If you really think the debate is worth having, politely respond by saying something like this: "I hear you, that's a good question. So we don't have tons of people jumping into the conversation, do you mind if I private message you and discuss it there?" If the answer is *Yes*, then go for it; if the answer is *No*, then don't engage in a discussion, or, at the very least, think and pray before you respond to each comment. A prayerless Christian on social media is a dangerous Christian. Whatever you do, don't be the person who goes on the attack. That's not Christian. That's anti-gospel. No Christian should act that way. We should be concerned about whether we're glorifying God or not.

SOCIAL MEDIA TO THE GLORY OF GOD

The apostle Paul tells us in 1 Corinthians 10:31 to do everything to God's glory: "So, whether you eat or drink, or whatever you do, do all to the glory of God." This includes how we conduct ourselves on social media. Like I said above, social media can be a great tool—it can also be used for evil things and reveal sin in the heart of a believer (or, worse yet, reveal that the believer is not truly a believer). Evidence of an immature heart in a Christian is seen by their conduct on social media.

With eternity on the line in everything we do, it's important to be wise in how we use social media. Just like no prayer is too small to ask God, so also no activity we do is less important in God's eyes as it relates to our witness. We can bolster our witness on social media; we can also severely damage it. Unfortunately, I think the latter has been true more than not.

If you struggle with social media usage and how to conduct yourself on it, you should do some serious praying and ask God to give you wisdom in how to proceed. He may answer by making it evident to you to delete your social media. Take a break at the very least. Your spiritual health—and others' spiritual health—is far more important than perusing social media.

CONCLUSION

To conclude this chapter, I will say this: one of the most important things you can do on social media is have a good understanding about whom you're speaking with, like I mentioned briefly earlier. This is why it's wise to not comment on controversial things because, many times, you might not know the other person. In that scenario, you don't know how they're going to respond and the conversation may escalate quickly. You also may deeply hurt somebody and assume their motives because you don't know them personally. This is why it's important to know your audience.

•••

{ 4 }

...

Knowing Your Audience

...

H ave you ever heard someone say, "Read the room, dude?" Well, that's what we're talking about in this chapter. In this chapter, we're going to address how to read the room when we're evangelizing.

A while back I watched a video of a Arizona pastor talking with a college student.[10] They had a cordial discussion over spiritual matters. Every now and then the pastor would point out that the student's worldview is inconsistent. The pastor was straightforward in saying that, though the student claims to believe that morality is subjective, he is also wearing a shirt that says, "Free Palestine."[11] The pastor not only showed him the inconsistency there (even if the student didn't see it) but also made a beeline for the gospel at the end of the conversation.

Why do I bring this up as an example? I do so because this pastor had to be blunt with this gentleman but he "[spoke] the truth in love" (Ephesians 4:15). Multiple times the pastor had to say things like, "You're being inconsistent," or "But

---

[10] Apologia Studios, "Pastor vs. Moral Nihilist," November 13, 2019, https://www.youtube.com/watch?v=UciOzJFTjc8.

[11] If morality is subjective, what's so good about freeing Palestine?

I know you don't believe that," or, even more, "I know you believe God is real." These things are tough to say but sometimes necessary. If said in the wrong way, they can make a good conversation turn bad. It's in these moments when we have to know our audience. In this particular conversation the pastor felt as though he could be more straight-forward with this student, whereas in other conversations he may not be as blunt. It simply depends on the audience.

Understanding the individual's personality plays a considerable role in ensuring we don't come across offensive. If you begin speaking with somebody and they come across as timid and non-confrontational, it's best to talk in a gentle, compassionate, and soft way. In other words, use your inside voice. In this example, there's probably no need to argue, but merely have a polite discussion. Of course, there is no formula to this. Don't make it all about reading the other person. Follow the Spirit's leading in how you will talk to them, and use your God-given intelligence. Sometimes you should be blunt and other times you should scale it back a bit.

GENTLY BLUNT

In 2016 I went on a mission trip to Provo, UT for outreach to Mormons. A couple of weeks later as we returned home, I was spending time with my then-girlfriend when, suddenly, there was a knock on the door. It was a Sunday afternoon so it was a bit odd. When I opened the door I saw two women and noticed they were LDS sisters. God, in His providence, had provided a gospel conversation at my girlfriend's doorstep a couple weeks after learning Mormon doctrine.

As I allowed them to talk, I told myself I needed to take this opportunity to be perfectly honest with them. Once they stopped, I asked them to explain the Mormon perspective of grace, salvation, Jesus, and the like. I knew I needed to say certain things that would deeply offend or upset them. And I did.

After I told them a few that things that were tough to say, one of them started to tear up. That pained me. The goal isn't to make somebody cry. Though I was gentle and soft-spoken, the truth of what I was saying was enough to make her upset. This illustrates something we need to understand when we share the gospel: you can be soft-spoken, gentle, and as compassionate as anyone, but the truth of the gospel will always offend. This truth doesn't negate the point of being gentle and compassionate, but it's a reminder that being gentle and compassionate doesn't save anybody.

Why do I tell this story? I don't use this example as a way to puff myself up; I simply use it as an example to show there are times to be soft-spoken and other times to be more upfront (like the Arizona pastor was at the beginning of the chapter). It all comes down to analyzing the situation, so to speak. You don't want to analyze too much or be too pragmatic, but it makes a difference. Ultimately, we do different things in order to glorify God in our witness.

I noticed that these two women were open to discuss the matters at hand, so I knew they wouldn't shut me down. Additionally, I knew that LDS people are usually very nice and well-tempered, which meant I could probably say a few things that were hard to hear for them but knew wouldn't make things escalate too much. More than anything, I knew I probably had this one conversation with them, so I had to proclaim the good news.

DON'T UNDERSTAND THE AUDIENCE

Like I said above, knowing your audience isn't some magical formula. Usually, if you're yielding to the Holy Spirit you will know how to speak, act, and respond. It will come naturally. So I am not saying to look intensely at the other person to figure out how to respond. At that point you may look a little bizarre. The Spirit will help; follow His lead. But many times we're not following the Spirit's guidance when we evangelize. We rely on our own smarts and not God's; Proverbs 3:5-6 gets thrown out the window. This is when we get offensive.

Part of understanding how to speak to another individual is recognizing the context. Where are you? Are you at a university, the local Planned Parenthood, or a busy sidewalk? Maybe you're simply sitting down with a friend for a cup of coffee. How you speak depends on the context and the person. This may seem like common sense, but on too many occasions we forget this key point.

Take for instance speaking with somebody—or many people—at a university. You go there every Friday morning when everybody is walking to class so you're likely to strike up a conversation with a lucky individual. How do you speak to them? No doubt, you need to come off as welcoming but after that it largely depends on how they speak to you first. Do they come off gentle and curious? Then be gentle and compassionate back. Do they come off as abrasive? At that point, I believe it's appropriate to calm them down first but also be very straightforward, yet with a calm tone. A blunt answer with a harsh tone won't solve anything, but a blunt answer with a calm tone might redirect the conversation. Of course, a student may walk past while screaming an expletive at you. Ignore it.

I don't mean to be the tone police—as I believe the culture places too much emphasis on tone—but it needs to be said: tone matters. You might have to say very difficult things, but if you do it in the correct tone, then the person will either be receptive or, at the very least, open to continuing the conversation. We shouldn't create tension or animosity with our tone. Our tone should be the thing that deescalates the conversation, not the opposite.

Let's pick another example: an abortion clinic. This is where violence is more likely to happen, so it's always important to pray for wisdom in this situation. Usually you have to elevate your voice when evangelizing at the abortion mill. That's all fine and good; just make sure it's legal (noise wise). We want to avoid any unnecessary confrontation with the authorities. That doesn't mean there won't be instances where we have to deal with them, but it shouldn't be a goal.

But regarding how we speak at this place, we have to again understand the context. Many times you will be raising your voice to people who get out of their car to walk inside. What do you do in that situation? You don't want to come across abrasive or rude but you do need your voice to be heard. Three words: Plead with grace. As a woman is walking into the clinic, the last thing they need to hear is a Christian shouting, "You're a murderer!" No, they need to hear something like, "That baby deserves to live! We will help you!" Something similar to that is appropriate. Plead with grace, not condescension.

You must ask yourself this question: Do I genuinely love people? If so, your voice should spring forth with compassion and heartbreak over the horrendous decision the mother is about to make. Your voice may be loud but your heart is full with compassion. Even more, make sure the end goal is the salvation of the mother (and anybody else involved). If you stop her from going inside for the abortion, but she is still lost, what good is that? Don't get me wrong, it's a huge win to save the baby, but let's preach the gospel, too.

Make sure they hear the love in your voice. Beckon them to come speak with you; tell them the good news of Jesus Christ. Have a heart full of compassion for them even in the midst of their rebellion. Plead with them and tell of the amazing sacrifice of Jesus. Show them that His burden is light.

It's very important to know your audience, which means understanding your surroundings. If I am not aware of the person I am talking to or the people in my general vicinity,

I may come off as offensive because I've failed to present the gospel in the right tone. For example, you don't want to walk into your local Starbucks with a megaphone and start yelling "Repent!" Not only would you be offensive and obnoxious, but you would also make things awkward. Do you really want to be *that person?* If you're in a coffee shop, grab your coffee, sit at a table, and be welcoming (Romans 15:7). There is an evangelist who has a cover on his laptop that says, "My name is Tony and I'm a Christian. Have any questions about spiritual matters? Have a seat. Let's talk!"[12] I think this is outstanding. It's like a glorified gospel tract. They walk past, see it, and can decide whether to come talk or not. All you do is sit, sip your coffee, and be welcoming.[13]

ARE YOU LISTENING?

There are myriad of ways to dampen the good news of the gospel with our attitude. One surefire way to do that is by not listening to the person. I think one of the reasons we do this is because we try to plan the conversation out in our head. We think, "If I say X, and they say Y, then I'll say Z," without realizing we should let the Holy Spirit dictate how the conversation is advancing. When this happens—whether intentionally or not—we are essentially shutting down the conversation because we have things to say and they just need to listen to us.

Sometimes the best thing we can do in evangelism is listen to the other person. I don't mean to say our words don't matter, since we all know they do. We know the gospel must be told. It must be proclaimed; people must hear the good news (Romans 10:14-17). The popular saying, "Preach the gospel; if necessary, use words," is completely and utterly false. Do I understand the sentiment? Sure. Our actions speak louder than words (we must practice

---

[12] See Tony Miano's website, crossencountersmin.com.
[13] Coffee with creamer, of course. Sorry, not sorry.

what we preach). However, our actions do not save souls—our words do. And it's not really our words, but the words of God.

So yes, the words we speak matter. With that said, my point is sometimes we get wrapped up in what we want to talk about rather than hearing the response from the other person. We talk over them; we stonewall them by quickly responding to them when they've just begun to respond to us. We do a disservice to the gospel because the person is thinking, "Is this the way Christians act?" No, it's not the way Christians should act when witnessing. We should humble ourselves, listen to what they have to say, and preach the gospel—using real words. Words of compassion, conviction, and unrelenting grace.

Moreover, listening shows that we want to know the person's story. It makes them feel more comfortable with opening up and describing their life. That's what we want, right? We want to witness to the gloriousness of the gospel, and one way we do that is hearing about other people's lives—the strife, turmoil, and anguish—and pointing them straight to the gospel. We get to tell them the good news they've needed to hear (or the good news they've continued to ignore)! That's the end game. But you can't get there, usually, if you don't turn your listening ears on.

So . . . listen.

WHEN IT GOES SOUTH

You can do all these things right. You can have the right tone, understand the audience, and display the love of Christ in the conversation—and sometimes the person will simply be in the mood for a confrontation. When that happens, stand your ground. I don't mean be rude back; I don't mean it's an excuse to be snarky. I mean stand firm on the gospel. Do not waver. All other ground is sinking sand and you've been commissioned by the Son of God to show people that!

Sometimes confrontation is necessary.

•••

{ 5 }

...

Confronting with Righteous Anger

...

In Matthew 21:12-13 we see Jesus acting not so Jesus-y. Culture, and some strange parts of evangelicalism, paints a picture of this happy-go-lucky Jesus who doesn't ever get angry and is always attempting to please everybody. This, in reality, is not the real Jesus. Shall we remind ourselves that Jesus is the Second Person of the Trinity? This means He was present with the Father in the Old Testament (along with the Spirit) for all the bloody stories, and must we remember the streets of blood in Revelation (Revelation 18:24)? Jesus isn't as cushy as you think He is.

With that in mind, we point our attention to Jesus in the temple. There were moneychangers in the temple who weren't concerned about the temple being a place of reverence and prayer but were only concerned about their own greed. When Jesus saw this, he flipped—literally. The text tells us that he "overturned the tables" and even "threw out all those buying and selling." Can you imagine watching Jesus do this? I'd certainly be paralyzed with fear that the divine Son of God, the Lord of glory, is showing just a little glimmer of His righteous anger toward sin. But it also shows us something else.

Being angry is not inherently bad.

In this passage we see directly from our Savior that one can be visibly angry and not sin. How is that? You are actually being like Jesus when you become upset over things that God hates. Confronting somebody over his or her sin does not mean you're being offensive. It means you're loving them the best way you can in that moment. Allow me to give you three examples.

PETER AND PAUL IN GALATIANS

There was a sticky scene going down in Galatians. Peter and Paul—two men that were radically transformed by the grace of God—had their own confrontation over the gospel. Before we delve into it, you should give it a read:

> "But when Cephas came to Antioch, I opposed him to his face, because he stood condemned. For before certain men came from James, he was eating with the Gentiles; but when they came he drew back and separated himself, fearing the circumcision party. And the rest of the Jews acted hypocritically along with him, so that even Barnabas was led astray by their hypocrisy. But when I saw that their conduct was not in step with the truth of the gospel, I said to Cephas before them all, 'If you, though a Jew, live like a Gentile and not like a Jew, how can you force the Gentiles to live like Jews?'"

Peter was not acting like he had been transformed by God's sovereign grace but was instead acting like he didn't know Christ. In this particular circumstance, you can make the case that Peter was, in fact, looking at the Gentiles with disdain. He was displaying partiality, which is a grievous sin (James 2:1-7). Paul noticed this and quickly confronted Peter—to his face.

The way Peter was acting prompted a necessary confrontation from Paul, a fellow brother in the faith. I'm sure Paul didn't enjoy it, but knew it was necessary for the sake of the gospel.

ABORTION

This abominable practice is rampant around the world, and the numbers of unborn children murdered grow by the minute in the United States. The legal slaughter of the most vulnerable among us has to be America's greatest sin; it has certainly provoked the judgment of God on our nation.

Does your blood not boil when you hear about the abortion statistics or when you hear a liberal politician try to convince others that abortion is healthcare? Does it "burn your biscuits" when abortion is still very legal even with technology like a 4D ultrasound and the ability to hear a heartbeat as early as six weeks? *This should make Christians angry.* And that's good and righteous. You should be angry; you should be upset at this atrocity. Quite frankly, if you're not angry about abortion, there is a problem. Righteous indignation to the sin of abortion is a godly response. Confrontation is necessary in this circumstance but always needs to be accompanied by grace. Let's take a look at another brief example.

FALSE TEACHERS AND GOSPELS

There's nothing more that upsets me when I see the gospel of Christ being distorted by the prosperity gospel hucksters of our day. From Kenneth Copeland to smiling preacher Joel Osteen, the gospel is being watered down and outright falsified on a daily basis. The sin of abortion is egregious; the sin of dismantling the gospel for your own gain is asinine. One issue deals with the image of God; the other deals with the work of Jesus. You can't mess with the gospel!

As Christians, we should be furious—but not too furious—when we see preachers twist the message of the gospel for their own greed. God delights in the salvation of sinners—bringing them from death to life!—and He hates when false prophets throw the message in the trash so they can pad their pockets. It is good and right for us to be angry when we see these things happen. We must confront others over preaching false gospels. It may be rather easy to criticize and make fun of these charlatans, but more than anything, it should cause righteous anger to swell up in our hearts.

But how we express that righteous anger *matters*.

WHEN RIGHTEOUS ANGER TURNS BAD

This is where things can get dicey, because our sinful nature often gets in the way of our righteous anger and turns it ugly. Even if, at first, we are displaying righteous indignation toward something, it is very easy to let that morph into sinful anger. That happens when we aren't slow to speak or to get angry (James 1:19). We may have godly anger and then start spouting off about it. Sometimes it's better to not say anything even if on the inside your blood is being cooked. That can certainly be a fruit of the Spirit—a sign of maturity in you. You may know that your anger is righteous and right but you're aware of where your mouth can take you if you let it fly. After all, we know that "whoever keeps his mouth and his tongue keeps himself out of trouble" (Proverbs 21:23). Learn to criticize without being aggressive. Learn to confront without being abrasive. Learn to be angry without sinning.

Another thing we have to be on guard about is dwelling on the particular circumstance too long. Whatever the situation may be—remember, it's a situation that causes righteous anger within you, which is a good reaction—it's important to not dwell on it. Dwelling on the situation can also turn your righteous anger into unrighteous anger. If you let it fester in your hearts, nothing good will happen. When we let frustrating situations linger within us, sin grows.

However, one of the biggest pitfalls in attempting to biblically display righteous anger is none other than the sin of *pride.* In this situation, it's not that we even get too angry. We wind up being prideful in our own ability to have righteous indignation. We begin to boast about having righteous anger and not even realize it. It may seem strange, but it's certainly a thing, and definitely in Reformed[14] circles. In our attempt to avoid unrighteous anger we fall into the pit of pride—a sin that God hates.

But let's go back to the main point here, that confrontation is sometimes necessary, definitely with righteous indignation. I've attempted to share with you some of the ways we are prone to fail in the midst of confronting somebody, but the main point is confrontation is needed sometimes.

CHRISTIANS GET OFFENDED TOO

Is it possible that our culture as a whole has become so feminized that we think *all* confrontation is about being offensive? Society is stalwart in its position to be offended by virtually everything. People are searching for something to be offended by because people love playing the victim. This is undeniably true because Christians do it too.

Do we remember a couple of years back when Starbucks came out with the Christmas cups that were red? Christians had meltdowns over it. There was one person who said "This . . . denies the hope of Jesus Christ and His story so powerfully at this time of year."[15]

What about a cup denies the hope of Jesus Christ? First of all, have we forgotten that Starbucks doesn't pretend to be

[14] Reformed is a shortened version of Reformed theology. This theology focuses on God's sovereignty as it pertains to salvation and how He governs the world.

[15] Hillary Hanson, Hillary, "Some Christians Are Extremely Un-happy About Starbucks' New Holiday Cups," Huffington Post, November 8, 2015, https://www.huffpost.com/entry/starbucks-red-cup-christmas-holiday-controversy_n_563f6e8fe4b0411d30715b15

a Christian organization? Second, and more importantly, are we taking the cup thing a *little* too seriously? Call me cynical, but I would venture to say the people most upset about the cups are the people who haven't been rightfully upset or taken action over far more important things like the destruction of marriage or the difference between a man and a woman. I guess it's easier to get heated about a cup than it is to be in godly uproar over the societal breakdown of the biblical structure of the family. Why is that? Because it's easier to get offended by something than to be the one offending.

Nevertheless, around-the-clock offensiveness is what we have to navigate as Christians. This is the world we live in now. If kneeling before a football game offends people then preaching the gospel of Jesus Christ is going to offend infinitely more. And in some situations, part of preaching the gospel might mean confronting somebody with grace.

Before I go any further, let me add a caveat. By confrontation, I don't necessarily mean you have to act like the manager of a baseball team getting up in the ump's personal space because of a blown call. That certainly involves sin. It has more to do with how straightforward you are and that you're not playing games anymore.

In this same regard, Jesus was done playing games with the Pharisees. He was done playing games with people who didn't care to play honestly.

OUR WITNESS AND LANGUAGE

In another scenario (and in many others), we see Jesus again confronting the Pharisees. However, in these confrontations Jesus wasn't flipping any tables but was also not mincing words when it came to how He felt about the Pharisees. Ponder these piercing words Jesus speaks to the Pharisees: "You brood of vipers! How can you speak good, when you are evil? For out of the abundance of the heart the mouth speaks"

(Matthew 12:34).

When Jesus called them "brood of vipers," He was point-ing out that they were deceitful, manipulative, wicked, and dangerous. If modern Christians were around when that hap-pened, they might've scoffed that Jesus used such harsh lan-guage and might've even told Jesus to repent. What we don't comprehend is that language isn't inherently evil. Yes, there is some language Christians should never use, like our mod-ern-day cuss words. We are told to not let any "foul language . . . come from your mouth, but only what is good for build-ing up someone in need, so that it gives grace to those who hear" (Ephesians 4:29). The fact that many Christians attempt to give a reason why cussing is permissible astonishes me. To me, this is a clear command to not use any bad language. It couldn't be more explicit, even in context.

It is quite evident that "brood of vipers" wouldn't fall in the category of foul language even though it's strong lan-guage. As Christians, we must not be afraid of using biblical language when we're having a conversation with somebody.

This is another issue that comes up: using strong language just because we can. I see this definitely within Reformed cir-cles for some reason. There's this inclination to use foul or strong language simply because it's deemed "cool," or because we have "liberty." That is quite silly. Not only might you be doing a disservice to your witness by using that language, but you're also being prideful in that you're using language like that *just because*. We know that "out of the abundance of the heart the mouth speaks" (Luke 6:45), so we must evaluate our hearts if we find ourselves being loose with our language.

Just because Jesus used *harsh* language doesn't give you the liberty to use *foul* language.

Bottom line: we must do a heart check when it comes to using strong language. What is our motive behind doing so?

Is it helpful to the context? Is it necessary? The questions shouldn't merely be "Is it sinful?" but "Is it beneficial?" I think it's hard to argue that using a four-letter word is ever beneficial to a conversation, let alone in the context of evangelism.

More importantly, will it glorify God? These are questions we should wrestle with, as we must remember to do everything—definitely speaking—to the glory of God (1 Corinthians 10:31). And how you answer will play a huge role in your witness.

We must remember context when thinking about using the language that Jesus did—or something similar to it. It's not always necessary. Imagine using foul language—or even harsh language—when having a conversation with a recent convert who struggles with cussing. What example are you setting? This goes back to thinking of others' interest before our own. Just because it's biblical doesn't make it helpful in a particular situation. Let me discuss for a moment when using strong language might be deemed helpful or warranted.

OPEN-AIR PREACHING AND LANGUAGE

Open-air preaching might be one of the hardest and most nerve-racking things to do. I have never done it personally. I believe you have to be a specific type of person or actually be called to open-air preaching. It's not a commandment of the Great Commission to open-air preach. But I digress.

In this form of preaching, you have to speak up. You're either projecting your voice or using amplification so people can hear you loud and clear. In this scenario, if you're preaching, I believe you're biblically warranted to say the words "Sons of hell," when referring to the lost world. That would be harsh language. Virtually nobody will react positively to it, and that's okay. You're speaking from the authority of the Bible—don't back down from that. Don't apologize for that. People, even many Christians, complain about street preachers (some deserve it), but we have to remind them that Jesus preached in the street. In our preaching we must be compassionate and extend grace but also bold and unwavering on the realities of sin. I think street preachers should use that phrase when referring to the dying world around us *in the proper context*. Again, you shouldn't say it merely because it's okay. But when you do, it might just grip the heart of one person who is on the fence.

Or it might just get you sucker-punched. But that's okay.

There are other street preachers who "deserve" to be sucker punched because they're preaching morality devoid of the gospel. *I am not saying be those types.* My point is to stand your feet firmly in the foundation of the gospel and preach your heart out and the Holy Spirit will direct your words.

CONFRONTING FRIENDS

Let me shift the focus here from our witness to our conversations with our brothers and sisters in Christ. Even among Christians there can be this stigma of never confronting anybody over sin. It's simply not true that we shouldn't confront brothers over sin. When necessary, we must confront other Christians over their sin, just like Paul did with Peter. The gospel mandates it. If a church is reflecting the biblical model, it will eventually happen.

To be quite honest, you're not a good friend if you don't confront another friend over his or her sin—that's not love, but cowardice. Yes, it will be difficult—definitely if they don't respond well. But it's unequivocally necessary. Even still, there's a way to confront and still be full of grace and compassion. Confrontation doesn't equal harshness. Confrontation isn't supposed to be void of grace; in fact, there should be more grace in your confrontation because of how serious the issue may be.

Even while confrontation is sometimes necessary, we need to be people who leak out grace and compassion because that's what Jesus did. In short, even in the midst of confrontation, even in the middle of having a difficult conversation, we need to be peacemakers.

{ 6 }

...

Be a Peacemaker

• • •

In the first chapter we went over the myriad of ways Christians add to the offense of the gospel (and have expounded on that in the chapters following). The last thing we want to do is make the gospel harder to believe because of our words and actions. Of course, the answer to this dilemma is not to be afraid of offending, but rather to humble ourselves under God's mighty hand (1 Peter 5:6). We must decrease and He must increase (John 3:30).

We should be known for our gentleness instead of our incessant need to be in the thick of things. We should be known for our compassion and peace rather than our obnoxious rhetoric.

In this chapter, I want to talk about the necessity for Christians to be peacemakers. Not troublemakers, riot-makers, or mischief-makers—but peacemakers. Out of all things, we should be known for our ability to keep the peace—when necessary.

BE AT PEACE WITH ALL MEN

The book of Romans has to be the greatest book in all of Scripture. Of course, it's not that it's actually better than other books since we know "all Scripture is breathed out by God" (1 Timothy 3:16), but Romans is littered with gospel truths and covers virtually every aspect of Christ's work.

The first eleven chapters of Romans detail specific doctrines like justification by faith alone, penal substitutionary atonement, and even Israel's relationship to the church. The rest of the chapters focus on Christian imperatives, that is, what Christians must do *in light of* what we've all heard. Chapters 1–11 are essentially saying, "Believe this," and the rest of the chapters are saying, "Now do this."

Toward the end of chapter 12 we see the apostle Paul name off what seems to be several individual to-dos. In verse 18 the apostle says, "If possible, as far as it depends on you, live at peace with everyone." There are many counter-cultural statements in the Bible, and this is one of them. In a day and age when it seems like everybody is at each other's throat—even Christians (just look on Facebook and Twitter)—this verse says to do the opposite. It goes against the natural inclination of humans.

We need a breath of fresh air—fresh air of peace among people. And this fresh air needs to be more prevalent in Christians. It starts with the body of Christ. Constant bickering isn't getting us anywhere. This may be an election year (written in 2020) — and tensions are high from racial issues and COVID-19—but that doesn't mean we succumb to the divisive madness.

God has commanded you to be a peacemaker. He has directed us to be people who are peaceful. Just like Jesus, we are to be compassionate. This goes a tremendous way in our witness to the gospel. But that comes with a caveat: peaceful doesn't mean cowardly.

PEACEFUL, NOT COWARDLY

When our minds think of a peaceful person, we automatically think of somebody who is afraid of confrontation or isn't willing to engage in debate. In short, we think of pacifists. However, being a peaceful Christian doesn't mean you shouldn't ever engage in arguments or even confront others when necessary, as we just went over. Occasionally it's your job as a fellow Christian to call out another Christian's behavior. You should not try to be peaceful so much that you don't follow the Spirit's leading to confront sin. At that point you're bordering on disobedience.

Think of Jesus, for example. He was the epitome of a peaceful person since He was without sin (Hebrews 4:15). This same Jesus also called the Pharisees white-washed tombs (Matthew 23:27) and flipped tables in the temple (Matthew 21:12–13). Jesus was perfect, so logically we can conclude that peaceful people have to conduct themselves in a bolder fashion to get a point across on occasion.

In the same way, there will be moments when you have to plant your feet firmly in the ground of the gospel and confront another Christian over his or her sin. It's not because you *want* to but because you *need* to—if you want to see that person become more like Jesus. Unchecked sin leads to dysfunction within the church and causes catastrophic problems. Many times Christians do not notice they are sinning, therefore it's up to you say something about it. Being a peaceful Christian doesn't mean you should never get involved in difficult situations; it simply means you shouldn't be the one causing them.

The key phrase in this verse is *as far as it depends on you*. You can't truly be at peace with everybody because not everybody wants to be at peace with you. Jesus told us this. If the world hated Him, they are surely going to hate us (John 15:18). Some people take pleasure in being at odds with others purely because they're Christians. Believe it or not, Christians act this way too.

Being peaceable—somebody who displays the fruit of the Spirit, essentially—is very important because it makes us more like Christ (Romans 8:29). There are three main ways to exercise this peacefulness in our lives, definitely as it relates to out witness: the local church, your community, and social media.

PEACE IN THE CHURCH

We know problems of division will arise within the local church because the church is made up of sinners. This is obvious. But it's problematic when you have members of a church who insist on not being peaceful. They antagonize, cause strife, and bring disunity. At some point you may bring church discipline into the conversation, though it's gut-wrenching to do so. And let me say this. *All churches should practice church discipline.* Not that you should want to, but the guardrails should be put in place when issues arise—because they will arise (dealing with sinners, remember?). A church that doesn't practice church discipline *when necessary* is nothing more than a Christian social club. *And divisive Christians thrive in those types of churches.*

It's one thing to struggle to be peaceful within your local church—we all may struggle with that on occasion because there's always something that will make us uncomfortable. It's another situation to enjoy causing an aroma of tension in your church. Something is wrong when controversy produces excitement in your heart. At that point, an endless amount of heart checking needs to be done. The local church is a place that should naturally have peacefulness, as Christians come together each week for a common pleasure: to worship God through preaching, songs, and fellowship while marveling at the resplendence of the gospel. This worship gets hindered when Christians within the church make it a goal to be divisive in every way. Unity is not optional.

If a church is to have a good witness in the community, it needs to be unified. When you're not peaceable even within your local church, you're not simply sowing discord among other Christians, you're also making it more difficult for the church to act like the church.

"How can one be a peaceful person within the church?" one may ask. Foundationally, it works when we *think of other people before ourselves.* This is the epitome of the humility that Jesus shows us in Philippians 2. See for yourself: "Have this mind among yourself, which is yours in Christ Jesus, who, though he was in the form of God, did not count equality with God a thing to be grasped, but emptied himself, by taking the form of a servant, being born in the likeness of men. And being found in human form, he humbled himself by becoming obedient to the point of death, even death on a cross" (Philippians 2:5–8).

Jesus, who is God Incarnate, descended to this earth in human flesh, humbled himself to the point of death—for you. Jesus emptied Himself. No, this doesn't mean He ceased being God; rather, it means He temporarily veiled his full glory He had with His Father before the world began. That, my friends, is humility.

If we have been born again, then we have the Holy Spirit within us. The Spirit *will* produce this type of humility in you. That doesn't mean it will be easy to think of others' interests before our own—it's our natural inclination not to—but it means you will become more like Jesus in your witness by the Spirit's power.

Additionally, this humility will be evident when we don't quarrel over secondary or tertiary doctrinal issues like baptism or eschatology.[16] We're at peace with others in the church because we know, even if we disagree on certain things, we all still love the same Jesus. There is no need for heated argumentation because we have the "same love" and "same mind" that is described in Philippians 2:2.

We have the responsibility as followers of Jesus to be harmonious with other believers within the church God has us

---

[16] Eschatology is the theological term for the study of end times.

in. Because we love Jesus, we should be the ones deescalating conflict, not starting conflict.

PEACE IN YOUR COMMUNITY

If you live in a small town, this statement applies even more. In a rural town, more people know you, which means more people know if you're peaceful or divisive. You can't hide it. If you're not at peace with everybody, your reputation will precede you. People will know to stay away because you create and nurture conflict.

Friends, understand the Bible is not asking you to simply be *at peace* with other Christians. It's mandating you to be at peace with *all* people—believers and unbelievers alike. You have no excuse. You may love other Christians in a different way than you do the rest of society, just as a husband loves his wife in a different way than his children. But you can't be peaceful in a different way. You need to be at peace with all men in the same way.

There are no ifs, ands, or buts about it.

The primary motivation for being peaceful is that it magnifies Christ. He sent us out to be fishers of men in a lost world. It does nothing good for you to act like the world while trying to bring the world to Christ. God certainly isn't glorified when we are always in the middle of a squirm.

Sometimes it's solely your attitude that gives people reason to scorn God and His church even more than they already do. What's worse is giving other Christians and/or unbelievers in your community a reason to affiliate your behavior with the local church you attend. In other words, your behavior has peripheral consequences. Being a peaceful Christian isn't primarily for your sake but for the sake of other Christians. Keep Philippians 2 in your minds. Let it get stuck in your head. Read it over and over until—like I have experienced with the Puppy Dog Pals theme song—you can't *not* think about it.

One of the qualifications for pastoral ministry is to have a good reputation with outsiders. Not just with your church or other Christians in the community, but with unbelievers. All people. Most of the qualifications for pastoral ministry apply to all Christians. We should all strive to have the pastoral characteristics. It's simply irresponsible as a Christian to look at the qualifications and think, "Those don't apply to me."

We can't glance over the qualifications of a pastor—*be above reproach, be the husband of one wife, be sober-minded, self-controlled, respectable, hospitable*, etc.—and say, "Eh, not being a drunkard is just too much for me," for instance. That's preposterous. Sure, some don't apply—but most do.

I encourage you to give 1 Timothy 3:1-7 a read and ponder if you fit those characteristics.

PEACE ON SOCIAL MEDIA

This one shouldn't be a doozy, friends, but it is. I can't begin to explain how many times I've seen Christians behave divisively on social media. It's everywhere. I see it everyday. It's hard to miss. It's simply harder to be peacemakers on social media because we don't have the blessing of seeing people in person. We get trigger-happy and post before we think.

I'm not saying Christians shouldn't use social media; even more, I'm not saying Christians shouldn't post, comment, and share controversial things. What I am saying, however, is what Romans 12:18 is saying. As far as it depends on you, Christian, be at peace with all people on social media.

Too many Christians don't think about the image they're portraying when they pounce on the hot-topic debate or make a Facebook post that they know will stir the pot. Our mouths shouldn't drool when somebody posts something controversial. Being a peacemaker doesn't mean never having interactions; it means knowing when to post and not to post. It means knowing the limits and knowing when to proceed. Sometimes it means having the discussion in private and not on the public thread.

BE AT PEACE

Whether it's in the local church, your community, or on social media, be intentional about being at peace with everybody. Because the gospel is at stake, we must know when to be gentle yet bold, compassionate yet firm, peaceful yet uncompromising.

We have been called to preach an offensive gospel while remaining peaceful as far as it depends on us. With the Spirit's power, we can. But sometimes we run into an issue. There are countless Christians who are unbalanced: they possess the truth of God but poorly display the love of God. In short, they have truth without love.

•••

{ 7 }

...

Truth Without Love

...

The church needs truth. In a day and age when there are many secular, anti-Christian ideas infiltrating the church, we need to stand all the more firm on the solid rock that is the Bible while holding fast to the unshakeable truths Christians have believed for over 2,000 years! We need truth, and that truth is Jesus (John 14:6). We are at a pivotal moment in history. Christians are marginalized, persecuted, and demeaned for what they believe. Not a day goes by that Christians don't have to take a strong stand for what they believe in.

As Christ's ambassadors, we must witness faithfully to the reality of Christ's perfect life, atoning death, and victorious resurrection! He lived a sinless life even though He was tempted in every respect as we are (Hebrews 4:15). In his death He atoned for all of the sins of His people as their substitute (2 Corinthians 5:21). He then rose victoriously on the third day for our justification (Romans 4:25). He crushed sin, Satan, and death in the process. Sin no longer has dominion over us because of Jesus (Romans 6:14). His death on the cross was the beginning of the end for Satan, the father of lies (Genesis 3:15; John 8:44).

Christians are who we are because of the finished work of Christ. It is our joy-filled duty to go into the world and show people their sin through the law and call them to repentance and faith, just as Jesus did (Mark 1:15). Make no mistake: we need truth. This God-given truth should not be forsaken for anything—not for the culture's carnal desire, your friends, or even for your family (Luke 14:26). Eternity is at stake and the world needs Christ—just as we do!

THE TRUTH ABOUT TRUTH

This is not a game for us. Christians cling tightly to the immutable truths found in Scripture like they're more precious than gold (Psalm 19:10). Nothing is as sweet as the finished work of Jesus Christ. Nothing, nada, zip. We stake our lives, integrity, and reputation on the truths of the gospel. Nothing can come between our beliefs in the gospel. And that's not because Christians are so intelligent and strong. Rather, it's because the God we serve is omniscient and omnipotent. He is all-knowing and all-powerful.

Christians are not the popular kids at school anymore. We're the freaks, the outcasts of society, the ones who get laughed at because we believe a man rose from the dead. And we're okay with it.

We believe every word that comes out of God's mouth through the pages of Scripture. Not one word is false. As a result, we affirm the essential truths of the Christian faith and go out into this lost and dying world to preach a message of hope, of forgiveness, of salvation. And we will *not* shy away from it.

That is the truth about the truth.

TOO FOCUSED ON TRUTH

But there's a problem. And the problem is why I wrote this book. In the Christian faith there are many people who know the right things but frequently do not say the right things—they don't consistently love others. These are usually the people who spout off something rude in the context and follow it up with, "I am simply trying to tell you the truth in love." They're getting the truth part correct, but the love part is nowhere to be found. In evangelism, this can be a huge problem because our lack of love seeps into the conversation.

Is it possible to be too focused on truth? It's possible to be too focused on anything. Any idea, physical thing, or sport—whatever—is possible to be focused on too much. This is called idolatry. We are so utterly depraved that we can take a doctrine of the faith and be so wrapped up in it that we've stopped believing it for the sake of knowing God but solely because it puffs ourselves up in knowledge (1 Corinthians 8:1). At that point, it's just feeding our ego. Believing these doctrines are only a means to an end, with that end being the knowledge of the one true God. It's astonishing that we can take a doctrine and make it into an idol. But we do it all the time.

Allow me to give you a real-life example. This person walked into a restaurant where he noticed a family who he knew had just lost their son. He approached the table to give his condolences and added, "Well, I sure hope he was a Christian."

To me, that's strike one. Though that is something you may think in your head, it's not something you should say out loud—definitely not in this context.

The family responded, "Yes, he was. He had been baptized and was a member of the Church of Christ." To which he responded, "Oh, no, if he did not repent of his sins and believe in Jesus, then he's in hell!"

Another strike. Again, this isn't about the truth of what he said. If somebody does not repent of their sin and believe in Jesus's finished work, they will go to hell. And correct, baptism does not save a person but is only an outward expression of an inward reality. But in this specific context, that's the last thing you should say to a *grieving* family. It rightfully made them very upset.

Unfortunately, believers cause other situations just like this. Why do we do this? Is it a lack of maturity? Is it a shallow understanding of the Bible? Is it just our personalities?

Foundationally, it's an issue with loving others.

THE LOVE CHAPTER

First Corinthians 13 is quite possibly the most popular chapter in the Bible. Many unbelievers know these verses and oftentimes use them when they see Christians behaving poorly. Whether it's at a wedding or in Sunday service, this famous chapter is bookmarked.

It's known for being called the "Love Chapter" because of its emphasis on love and the Christian. In context, the apostle Paul is writing to the church at Corinth, which had been behaving in a not-so-Christian manner. In this chapter, Paul is making reference to spiritual gifts like tongues, prophecy, words of knowledge, etc. and is explaining to that church that you can possess all these gifts, but if you don't have love, you're nothing.

With that being said, the chapter still applies here for what we will be talking about. So let's explore the Love Chapter a little bit.

THE WAY OF LOVE

Before I get into anything else, I want you to read 1 Corinthians 13:1–7. So read it. The apostle Paul writes:

> "If I speak in the tongues of men and of angels, but have not love, I am a noisy gong or a clanging cymbal. And if I have prophetic powers, and understand all mys-

teries and all knowledge, and if I have all faith, so as to remove mountains, but have not love, I am nothing. If I give away all I have, and if I deliver up my body to be burned, but have no love, I gain nothing.

Love is patient and kind; love does not envy or boast; it is not arrogant or rude. It does not insist on its own way; it is not irritable or resentful; it does not rejoice at wrong-doing, but rejoices with the truth. Love bears all things, believes all things, hopes all things, endures all things."

True, biblical love is lacking within the Christian church today. Truth is there but love is not in many places. Christians place such an emphasis on truth that they forget love.

Just think of the first verse in the chapter: "If I speak in the tongues of men and of angels, but have not love, I am a noisy gong or a clanging cymbal." Insert something else at first like: "If I believe in substitutionary atonement, but have not love, I am a noisy going or a clanging cymbal." In other words, we may believe the right things, but we're also obnoxious because our speech is not "seasoned with salt" (Colossians 4:6). Our odious behavior drowns out our knowledge. Nobody cares to listen because we come across so condescending. Our words show that we don't really love them but just want to hear ourselves talk.

If we don't have love, we are nothing. All of our knowledge, whit, and deep theological discussions mean nothing if we don't display the love of Jesus. Who are we trying to impress? God is certainly not impressed.

REASONS WHY LOVE IS ABSENT

Christians are so disgruntled with the world's redefinition of love that they've strayed so far away from it and missed the biblical definition as well. Just as people make a god in their own image, many Christians make up their own definition of love. As a result, many churches are spilling over with Christians who know about God but don't *know* God.

Make no mistake: our society does, in fact, have a distorted view of love. It's a love that is merely an emotion and is depicted as something that ebbs and flows. We say, "I love you," to others but rarely mean it because our actions don't back it up. It's analogous to one of the Christmas episodes of *The Office* where Michael Scott says: "Presents are the best way to show someone you care. It is like this tangible thing that you can point to and say, 'Hey man, I love you this-many-dollars' worth.'"

To be sure: *The Office* is my favorite show of all time; my wife and I watch it on repeat. But what Michael said is obviously hilarious because that's not what it means to love others.

Moreover, we've convinced ourselves that we truly love others, but in reality we miss the mark many times—the simple definition of sin. One of the most unsavory things we can do is be a complete nincompoop to somebody and then say, "I am saying all this in love." I alluded to this earlier. This is a famous Christian cop-out so that Christians can be insensitive to others and then pretend we're being loving.

The frustrating thing is we know the biblical definition of love and still struggle with displaying it. It's frightening because we're all capable of this madness. We're all capable of believing one thing and doing another. Accompanied by repentance, this is simply a key part of the Christian life. Christians need to repent daily. We will go through times when we don't love very well. Other times, loving people will come more naturally. That is simply the up-and-down ride of the Christian life.

THE WHY

Why do we do this? The aching cry of our sin-stained hearts is the need to love all people, yet when it comes to real life, we stumble. Why, oh why, does this happen?

To put it succinctly: sin. Our sin gets in the way. Whether we have a natural inclination to be abrasive, cynical, or insensitive—these things are difficult to mortify if we don't actively strive, by the Spirit, to put those things to death (Romans 8:13). When cynicism is our normal, we should pray to the Lord to change our normal to compassion.

Christians must strive daily to kill the sin in their hearts that causes them not to love like Jesus loves. If we don't, we will have an ineffective witness. There's a great exercise we can do to not only convict us but also push us to biblical, Jesus-like love.

INSERT YOUR NAME

Staying with the theme of 1 Corinthians 13, there is an old trick that people do to measure if they love well. All you do is replace the word *love* with your name in the text when it says, "Love is patient, love is kind . . ."

It would look like this: "Blake is patient, Blake is kind, Blake does not envy or boast; he is not arrogant or rude. Blake does not insist on his own way; he is not irritable or resentful; he does not rejoice at wrongdoing, but rejoices with the truth. Blake bears all things, believes all things, hopes all things, endures all things."

Do you want to bring needed conviction in your life? Read those verses and insert your name. By my estimation, I am not patient or kind enough; I envy too much and sometimes I boast in myself rather than Christ. There are times when I am arrogant or rude, unfortunately. You get the point.

With that being said, we should not fall too deep into despair, because the beauty is that Jesus is all these things *perfectly*. You can read it like this: "Jesus is patient, Jesus is kind, Jesus does not envy or boast; He is not arrogant or rude. Jesus does not insist on His own way; He is not irritable or resentful; He does not rejoice at wrongdoing, but rejoices with the truth. Jesus bears all things, believes all things, hopes all things, endures all things." And the even better part: if you are born again, you have His righteousness—so when God looks at you, He sees Jesus!

DYING ON THE WRONG HILLS

One last thing I want to discuss before moving on is something that Christians don't think about too much: which theological hills to die on. This is a big issue within the church that nobody mentions often enough, but it causes massive division.

"Sometimes," Gavin Ortlund, Senior Pastor of First Baptist Church in Ojaj, CA, penned, "we have flattened out all doctrine—either because we want to fight about everything or because we want to fight about nothing."[17] The issue Ortlund is referring to is Christians forget what doctrines are essential and non-essential. Said another way, there are primary doctrines, secondary doctrines, and tertiary doctrines (maybe there are more categories).

When we become people who are constantly arguing about non-essential doctrines by making them more important than they are, we are offensive—not just to the outside world but, more importantly, to our own brothers and sisters in Christ. Making the gospel more offensive by our behavior may primarily be an issue when witnessing to unbelievers, but it has implications within the body of Christ as well.

When you behave this way, you may have truth, but you don't have love—or at the very least aren't showing it well. But what if it's the opposite? What if you love people, per se, but don't have God's truth? Buckle up: we will explore this in the next chapter.

---

[17] Gavin Ortlund, *Finding the Right Hills to Die On: The Case for Theological Triage* (Wheaton, IL: Crossway, 2020), 18.

{ 8 }

...

Love Without Truth

...

Think for a moment. Have you ever encountered someone who is what people call a *Yes* man? This person is, simply put, a people pleaser. He or she is not interested in anything else other than affirming you—or anybody else for that matter. They only make you feel good about yourself and never criticize or point out your flaws. He or she would never say one bad thing about you because he doesn't want to hurt your feelings. In short, this person only relates to you on the basis of "love."

What good is it for a person to only relate to others on the basis of love? We know, we know—love is extremely important, as it should be. As we covered in the last chapter, when love is absent, things turn ugly. But don't we need truth in our lives? Isn't truth important? If somebody only affirms and never criticizes you, then the elephant in the room must be pointed out: is that even love?

This prevailing attitude is part and parcel with the culture we live in today. Only affirmation, no denunciation; only words of acceptance, never rejection. Truthfully, it's a culture full of weaklings. I don't mean that in an insulting manner, but simply as a matter of reality. It's no wonder society has a hard time with criticism, given how our culture only wants to point out the good in others and never challenge in any way. It's a foreign concept.

We see this attitude in the ilk of liberal Protestantism.

LIBERAL PROTESTANTISM

In J. Gresham Machen's classic work *Christianity and Liberalism* he writes the following: " . . . the great redemptive religion which has always been known as Christianity is battling against a totally diverse type of religious belief, which is only the more destructive of the Christian faith because it makes use of traditional Christian terminology. This modern non-redemptive religion is called 'modernism' or 'liberalism.'"[18]

What Machen penned in 1923 remains prophetically true today: liberal Protestantism is an entirely different religion from Christianity. It's not difficult to see, though may be difficult to hear for some. You may have a harder time finding what those churches believe based on their statements of faith, but if you attend their services and hear their sermons, you'll quickly find out they're not orthodox.

What makes liberal Protestant churches not orthodox? Isn't it okay to be a little liberal in areas and still be a Christian? It depends on what we mean. Let me give you three areas that reveal these churches not to be orthodox: abortion, LGBTQ-related issues, and the Bible itself.

THE SACRAMENT OF ABORTION

The majority of liberal Protestant churches embrace the pro-abortion view. They have bought into the satanic lies of the emerging culture that coins euphemisms such as "repro-

---

[18] J. Gresham Machen, *Christianity and Liberalism*, new ed. (Grand Rapids: Eerdmans, 2009), 2.

ductive rights," "the right to choose," and "clump of cells."
It's barbaric, and these churches are going along with it. They
celebrate it, champion it, and advocate for the murder of children in mother's wombs.

Make no mistake: a church that firmly embraces that abortion is morally okay is not morally upright in the eyes of God.
That view is incompatible with the Christian worldview. You
can't have your cake and eat it too. Some may be put off or
offended by that. That's okay. Scripture is simply too clear to
beat around the bush on the slaughter of little ones made in
His image.

LGBTQ-AFFIRMING

Liberal Protestant churches are also very welcoming to the
LGBTQ community. To be frank, you can say the same thing
for conservative churches. We open the doors of the church
to all people—no matter the ethnicity, sexuality, gender, etc.
But with liberal churches, they don't simply open the doors,
but approve of them. They believe that homosexuality is not
a sin and that God deems them "holy," as one popular progressive author said.[19] Not only is homosexuality okay now,
it's also "holy." This is anti-Christian and goes directly against
God's good design.

In an attempt to appeal to all people, liberal churches are
embracing every person just as they are and proclaiming,
"You don't need to change!" This is untrue, of course. People
don't simply need to change but need to be born again (John
3:3). They need a new heart. Any church that denies or ig-
nores that isn't a true church.

---

[19] Diana Chandler, "Lifeway Pulls Hatmaker Books Over LGBT Views,"
Baptist Press, October 27, 2016, https://www.baptistpress.com/resource-li-
brary/news/lifeway-pulls-hatmaker-books-over-lgbt-views/.

FOUNDATIONAL ISSUE

Undergirding the erroneous views on abortion and other cultural issues is a profane disdain for sacred Scripture. Liberal Protestant churches reject the Bible as truth. They may pushback against that but their record speaks for itself. Why do they reject the teachings of the Bible? Because they reject God. They may believe in God (some churches don't necessarily believe in God anymore!), but they don't believe God. Their attempt to gain the approval of outsiders will eventually be seen as futile on the last Day when God shows them His disapproval.

They do not take Scripture seriously. Fruitless attempts are made to disprove or push away the Bible's clear commands as it relates to gender, sexuality, the image of God in the unborn, etc. Their problem is not conservative Christianity. Their problem is with God Himself, who wrote the Bible. Their refusal to bow the knee to God is evident through their worldly attempts at love.

PHONY LOVE

Many professing Christians who want to be accepting of all people proclaim that "love is love"—the slogan of the LGBTQ movement. But that's not acceptance. That's not love. That's enablement.

Enablement of sinners sends people to hell. Period. They proclaim love at the expense of truth. There are two things wrong with that. First, if you don't possess biblical truth, you don't possess biblical love. Their love is a phony love; truthfully, it's satanic. Second, liberal churches don't have a firm basis for truth. They are embracing the "progression" of culture and following the "truth is relative" mantra. So there goes truth, too.

Bigger than the issue of relative truth is that these churches forsake the objective truth of God—the truth that God is the

Creator of the universe (Genesis 1:1), humans rebelled (Genesis 3), and that He sent His Son to die for the world (John 3:16). They proclaim the love of God but ignore the wrath of God.

The words *sin* and *hell* are heresies in the liberal church.

At the foundational level, people who have "love" at the expense of truth are idolaters. They have created a god in their own image—a god to suit their own feelings. This god is all love and no wrath. This god doesn't punish the wicked and gives a pass to the vilest of sinners. That's not love. That's injustice.

In liberal Christianity, God only has one attribute: love. And because of this idolatrous view of God, they consequently do not have the right Jesus, either. Friends, there is nothing admirable about that.

Not only do they not have truth, but they also don't have love.

IN EVANGELISM

How does this all relate to the Christian's witness in the public arena? Surely we understand that an orthodox Christian possesses truth, so this may not be an issue. This is certainly true. Orthodox Christians won't have this issue, but we can struggle with compromising due to fear of man.

When we witness to others, we may be fearful of the reaction we receive and could be tempted to lie about what we believe in order to be more appealing. We cannot succumb to that temptation. This issue is going on inside the walls of Christ's church. Whether there are Christians with erroneous views or simply compromising the gospel message, possessing love but not truth can be an obstacle on occasion.

Church, this comes down to not forsaking truth. Jesus went through hell and back and promised to never forsake us.

The least we can do in our witness is be faithful to the Lord in how He has revealed Himself.

WHEN YOU FORSAKE TRUTH

There are countless Christians in the evangelical church who compromise the gospel in order to "love" others. We should not forsake the truth of God at the altar of so-called love. When you lose the truth because you're so focused on "just loving people," you wind up not having real love anyway. Real love doesn't hide from the truth. And this remains true definitely in gospel conversations. How can we be an effective witness when we don't believe the word we're trying to share?

When we forsake truth in order to love, we have shown that we care more about the approval of the culture than the approval of God. This is what Paul was saying in Galatians: "For am I now seeking the approval of man, or of God? Or am I trying to please man? If I were still trying to please man, I would not be a servant of God" (Galatians 1:10).

As Christians, it's impossible for us to please both man and God. If we are pleasing God, we are consequently not pleasing man; if we are pleasing man, then you best believe we're not pleasing God.

So the question is: who would you rather please?

"I JUST WANT TO LOVE PEOPLE"

There's a popular phrase that professing Christians use frequently. "I just want to be a Christian who is about love," they say. "I just want to love people." Absolutely. Amen. That couldn't be more true! However, most of the time this is in the context of downplaying theological truth. In order to appeal to others and look less offensive, Christians show how much they "love people" by enabling others in their sin. You're not loving but pushing them further down the road to hell. In attempting to show you're a loving person, you're actually doing the most unloving thing you can do: approving of their sin.

In progressive Christianity—which is the result of love without truth—there is no hope, joy, or peace. There is no foundation to stand on other than flimsy feelings that change as the culture shifts.

CONCLUSION

In these last two chapters, you may be wondering how these apply directly to the Christian's character in evangelism. As a review, let's briefly go over both.

When you possess truth without love, you are more prone to come across offensive to the person you're witnessing to. You may behave in an abrasive fashion or maybe you have a difficult time showing empathy. Either way, you may know the truth of God but struggle with showing the love of God.

When you possess love without truth, there's much more reflecting that needs to be done. Do you believe the truth of God's Word? Do you believe the historical, essential tenets of the Christian faith? If so, maybe think about if you're too willing to compromise your convictions in evangelism because you're focusing so much on loving others. When you elevate so-called love at the expense of truth, you may not be offending the culture, but you are now offending the one you don't want to offend: God.

WE NEED THE HOLY SPIRIT

Lord, give us some Christians who know truth and have love. Give us some Christians who can speak the truth in love (Ephesians 4:15). Give us some Christians who rely wholly on the power of the Holy Spirit to help them be an effective witness to the gospel of the Lord Jesus Christ.

•••

{ 9 }

...

A Supernatural Witness

...

Christians are supernatural creatures. The Bible echoes this in 2 Corinthians 5:17, "Therefore, if anyone is in Christ, he is a new creation. The old has passed away; behold, the new has come." Christians are people who have been made new. We are a people who, by the sovereign grace of God, possess both truth and love.

Outside of Christ, there is one person on this planet who displayed truth and love similar to Jesus. That person is none other than the apostle Paul. In his life he consistently affirmed God's unchanging, unshakeable truth and displayed God's sacrificial love. "One cannot think of Paul without a sense of admiration and wonder at the ways in which the Lord Jesus Christ used him in the lives of God's people," Guy Prentiss Waters said in his book *The Life and Theology of Paul*. "He is one of the greatest minds ever to have graced the Christian church."[20]

PAUL, AN EXAMPLE

The apostle Paul was unashamed of the gospel of Jesus Christ (Romans 1:16). He was utterly gripped by the truth God re-

---

[20] Guy Prentiss Waters, *The Life and Theology of Paul* (Sanford: Reformation Trust, 2017), 3.

vealed to Him on the road to Damascus (Acts 9:1–19). This piercing and eternal truth turned him from a terrorist against Christians into a lover of Christians. From a man who murdered believers to a man who pleaded with sinners *out of love* to turn from their sin and believe in Christ—the apostle Paul was made new by the grace of God! If God saved Paul, He can save anybody.

Paul the apostle told the church at Corinth to be "imitators of me, as I am of Christ" (1 Corinthians 11:1). And this is exactly the same thing we should do today. He knew that a supernatural witness meant possessing both truth and love, which he wrote about in Ephesians 4:15.

"Rather, speaking the truth in love," Paul said, "we are to grow up in every way into him who is the head, into Christ." I want to look at two aspects of this verse that are of utmost importance as it pertains not only to our witness but also to our sanctification as a Christian.

CONTEXT IS KEY

We frequently hear this phrase ("speaking the truth in love") by Christians, but do we know what it means practically? How do we faithfully walk it out? Before we consider the practical implications of this phrase, let's take a look at the context, which will bring to light other important things— things we experience on a daily basis.

Previously in the passage the apostle Paul is explaining what is known as the "fivefold ministry" to some Christian denominations, which is that God gave us the "apostles, the prophets, the evangelists, the shepherds and teachers."[21] What is the main reason God implemented these? The text tells us

---

[21] It's important to note that the term "fivefold" ministry is problematic because this means that all churches should have each of these ministry workers. However, that can't be true, since there are no longer apostles and prophets.

in the next verse: "to equip the saints for the work of ministry, for building up the body of Christ" (v. 12).

The reason God created these ministers is twofold: one, to equip all Christians for the work of the gospel and two, to edify, or build up, the church. The goal is for ministers to equip Christians and edify them deeply enough that "[they] all attain to the unity of the faith and of the knowledge of the Son of God, to mature manhood, to the measure of the stature of the fullness of Christ" (v. 13).

Ultimately God gave the church gospel ministers in order for us to "grow in the grace and knowledge of our Lord and Savior Jesus Christ" (2 Peter 3:18). And the more we know Jesus Christ, the more mature in the faith we will become ("mature manhood").

And here we come to the preceding verse of "speaking the truth in love." In verse 14, the apostle tells us, "so that we may no longer be children, tossed to and fro by the waves and carried about by every wind of doctrine, by human cunning, by craftiness in deceitful schemes." Increasing in the knowledge of Jesus Christ—and, in turn, the whole counsel of God—means no longer being infants in the faith. This is important, since as we grow out of Christian toddlerhood, we will no longer be swayed by other unbiblical doctrines, as Paul indicates. In other words, we will be able to discern biblical from unbiblical.

In the church today there are Christians who do not have a strong desire to study doctrine. This is discouraging because any Christian, by definition, is a theologian. We all don't have to be scholars but we must be workers. We must have the desire to learn more about God. When we are ministered to in a biblical manner, we will see when "every wind of doctrine" comes our way and know which is right or wrong.

Paul also writes to us about human cunning and craftiness in deceitful schemes. Essentially, Paul is referring to the false teachers who are doing the work of ministry for their own gain. They are not for you, and they certainly aren't on God's team. They are deceivers and liars. If we stay in toddlerhood Christianity, we will be vulnerable to these charlatans. These are people like Joel Osteen, Benny Hinn, Kenneth Copeland, and other popular false teachers. For the sake of yourself and the church, stay away from their teachings, as they are not for you but themselves.

SPEAKING THE TRUTH IN LOVE

Now that I am done with my rather-quick exegesis, we can look deeper into what speaking the truth in love means. In this passage, speaking the truth in love is contrasted with "human cunning by craftiness and deceitful schemes." In other words, those out there who use human cunning, deceit, and other forms of manipulation do not love you, though they may tell you that.

A person who loves you speaks truth no matter how difficult it is to hear. That is the epitome of speaking the truth in love. And here's the unfolding of the last part of this text: speaking the truth in love reveals that we are growing more and more into the likeness of Jesus Christ ("we are to grow up in every way into him who is the head, into Christ").

Jesus spoke the truth in love perfectly. Think back to the chapter on confrontation being necessary in certain situations. Do we believe Jesus was speaking the truth in love when He called the Pharisees white-washed tombs? Do we believe John the Baptist was speaking the truth in love when he lambasted the Pharisees by calling them brood of vipers? Do we believe the apostle Paul spoke the truth in love when he confronted Peter in Galatians?

Even more, do we believe Jesus, the disciples, and all Christians everywhere speak the truth in love when they call sinners to repent and believe (Mark 1:15)? I hope you answer those questions with a resounding "Yes!"

You see, our culture has redefined truth and love. They have pit truth and love against each other. They claim Christians are bigots and, because of what we believe, we're not loving anybody. Yes, this is true because they have changed the definition of love. In the culture's eyes, love equals approval and truth means nothing. They have forsaken the truth of God for their own perverted version of love. And if somebody doesn't accept their new version, they are "cancelled."

What society doesn't understand—or worse, what they deny—is that truth and love are *eternally* connected. They are intertwined; you cannot separate them. This has been the entire point of the last three chapters: Christians must possess both truth and love. It will come natural for Christians. Truth and love complement each other.

Truth points to love. This is clearly seen in 1 Timothy 1:5, which says: "The aim of our charge is love that issues from a pure heart and good conscience and a sincere faith." The point of charge (truth) is to have love from a pure heart. In other words, friends, learning the truth of God should lead you to love fellow image-bearers of God. In this verse, truth is not the goal but the means through which we are able to express true love. You need truth—don't be mistaken. Like I have said, it's impossible to have love without the truth.

At the same time, love supports truth. It rejoices with the truth. "Love does not rejoice in unrighteousness," Paul says in 1 Corinthians 13:6, "but rejoices with the truth." Love is glad when truth is spoken. Even more, love is ecstatic when truth is cherished and believed. Conversely, it is sorrowful when falsehoods are repeated. Love hates lies.

Like repentance and faith, truth and love are married, so to speak. They are inseparable, two sides of the same coin. They go together like PB&J. And there is an all-out war on both of them, and this is what Christians are facing today. This is why, in order to glorify God in your witness—and simply in your life as a Christian—you need truth and love. You need the knowledge of God in your head and the love of God in your heart. Said another way, the truth you learn needs to penetrate your heart—not just your noggin.

TRUTH AND LOVE IN WITNESSING

In order for me to make the point of this book come full circle, I had to veer off a little bit in order to show you the foundation of Christ-like character, which is what we've been talking about: truth and love.

Possessing truth and love means there will be times you are required to say hard things to people. If you love people like Jesus does—if you care for their souls—you will say difficult things. Many times this means telling people that if they don't rest in the finished work of Christ then they are headed for hell, fiery torment, suffering eternally under the wrath of God.

That is the most loving thing you can do.

Make no mistake: most people will not like what you say. Most people will be offended; some will become violent; few will actually take your words to heart. That is evangelism for the Christian. However, we shouldn't step back because of this possibility. (I will talk about that in the conclusion.)

Truth and love demand that we proclaim the whole gospel—even the parts that are unpopular. You see, most people don't have a problem with Jesus dying on the cross until they are told why He did. Things get awkward when a person realizes Jesus died because they are . . . sinners.

WHY PEOPLE GET OFFENDED

Some people are fine with labeling themselves a sinner, but it almost always comes with self-justification. You hear things like, "Yes, I am sinner—but so is everybody else!" or "Yes, I sin, but that doesn't make me a bad person." No, friend, that does literally mean you're a bad person. Like the late RC Sproul said: "We are not sinners because we sin. We sin because we are sinners."[22] You can't turn the sinner switch on and off. You are a sinner by nature. It's our DNA, so to speak. It's what came most natural to us before Christ.

This is why it's extremely important for us to display Christ-like character in evangelism. We don't need anything else getting in the way of the gospel's offensive message, which *is* offensive to people—it exposes them for who they truly are: wicked sinners in need of a Savior. Most people believe they are good by nature. This is because they compare themselves to the world. If I compare myself to Hitler, I am a very righteous person. But that falls short of the issue at hand. What I need to do is compare myself to perfection—Jesus Christ. When I compare myself to Jesus, I fall woefully short. All people fall short (Romans 3:23).

There is no more "My good outweighs my bad." You have no good (Romans 3:10).

There is no more "God is a forgiving God, so I am sure I will be just fine." Though God does forgive, He by no means acquits the guilty (Exodus 34:7).

And because Christians love others, we are compelled by God to tell people the bad news of their sin. We will be faithful in showing others they are guilty before God just as we

---

[22] @RCSproul (RC Sproul). "We are not sinners because we sin. We sin because we are sinners." Twitter. 3 October, 2017, 11:18 AM. https://twitter.com/rcsproul/status/915249707974365184?lang=en

once were. But then we point them straight to Jesus—the human embodiment of truth (John 14:6) and love (1 John 4:8).

Friends, this is why it's imperative to speak the truth in love. We must have truth; we must contend for the truth; we must not compromise on the truth. The truth is absolutely necessary.

THE NECESSITY OF TRUTH

Sadly, we live in a society where people believe truth is relative. What does it mean for truth to be relative? Basically, to believe that truth is relative is to say that truth merely hinges on personal preferences or societal structures. In other words, truth is not true everywhere or for all people. It's not absolute. Allow me to give you a very simple example.

I believe that 2 + 2 = 4. Another person believes that 2 + 2 = 5. The other person believes we can both be right. Why? Because to them the rightness doesn't depend on an objective standard of truth but merely the sincerity of belief.

Friends, that is *absolutely* wrong. The sincerity of one's belief doesn't automatically make the belief true. You can strongly believe you will fly if you jump off a skyscraper, but the reality is you'll plummet to your death. Sincerity doesn't equal reality.

In his book *The Moment of Truth*, Dr. Steven Lawson talks about eight points of truth.

1. Truth is divine; that is, all truth originates with God.

2. Truth is absolute; that is, truth reigns as the highest authority in all matters.

3. Truth is objective; that is, truth is propositional and has precise meaning.

4. Truth is singular; that is, it's cohesively one system and is one entity.

5. Truth is immutable; that is, God does not change and neither does His truth.

6. Truth is authoritative; that is, what's in His Word is supremely authoritative.

7. Truth is powerful; that is, it cuts deeply, both convicting and challenging us.

8. Truth is determinative; that is, it dictates how you live your life.[23]

Lawson is candid about the importance of the truth. He knows that the truth is a matter of life and death. "The truth, the whole truth, and nothing but the truth," he said, "this is our most noble pursuit in this world."[24]

We should be truth pursuers, which means we should be Christ pursuers. And this truth we pursue—where do we find it? We find it in Jesus, of course. But where do we see Jesus? We look no further than Scripture. We see God's truth in God's Word. Christians must be people who bathe in God's Word and believe its truth!

THE NECESSITY OF LOVE

Like I said before, we can have all the truth in the world—we can know many great things about God and how He works—but if we do not have love for others in our hearts, it's all in vain. It's pointless. The Bible tells us we are to love our neighbors as ourselves (Mark 12:31). There are two things in this verse that are extremely important.

First, God isn't asking us to simply love our physical neighbors. He doesn't want us merely loving the people close to us. Our neighbors are everybody. God commands us to love all

---

[23] Steven Lawson, *The Moment of Truth* (Sanford: Reformation Trust, 2018), 9–16.

[24] Ibid, 19.

people—no matter the ethnicity, gender, sexuality, etc. This means we can't look at somebody and say, "I don't care about you." God cares about them, so you should as well.

Even more, loving your neighbor means loving people you disagree with and/or find annoying. Love doesn't discriminate; that is, it's to be applied to all people with genuine affection. The love we've been told to give to others is not grounded on common interests or similar stories. It's an agape love—a sacrificial love. A love that Jesus showed.

Second, we are to love others as we love ourselves. What's the point here? The point is that we love ourselves so much, so we should be loving others with the same amount that we love ourselves. Better yet, the Bible teaches us to look out for others' needs before our own, as that's what Jesus did by going to the cross (Philippians 2:1–11). That is the greatest example of humility we find in the Bible. But it's also an amazing example of love.

We are to be people driven by the truth of God that is wrapped in the love of God.

And this is not some cushy, Hallmark-type love. It's not the love you have for a great, juicy steak. It's not a love you have for your team winning the Super Bowl.[25] It's a love of sacrifice. This is part of the issue—even with Christians. As believers, we may sometimes have a distorted view of love. We have bought into the world's definition of love that is controlled by ever-changing emotions. To be sure, emotions are obviously a part of love, but love is not mere emotions.

THE LOVE OF COMPLACENCY

There are at least two different types of love. Right here I want to talk about the love of complacency, which is the love you have for ice cream or something else that's delicious (I

[25] I wouldn't know anything about the Super Bowl. I'm a Vikings fan. It's rough out here.

referenced this briefly before). This is the love the world of-
fers. It's love that won't get you through the good times and
bad. It's a love that won't allow you to look past the faults of
others. It's a love that doesn't cover a multitude of sins (1 Peter
4:8). It's a love that, ultimately, is still about you.

The foundational issue here is that this type of love is based
on the loveliness of the object. Pizza has to taste good for me
to love it. Ice cream needs to be sweet for me to enjoy it. Steak
needs to be juicy for me to find it delicious. Unfortunately,
this is the same type of love many people have for others. It's
a love that is rooted in how other people behave. In short, it's
a transactional love. (Maybe this is why America's divorce rate
is 50 percent!)

The love of complacency is not what God calls you to. He
doesn't want you to love people based on their loveliness. If
that were the case, there would be no such thing as love. So
how does He want us to love others?

THE LOVE OF BENEVOLENCE

Contrasted with complacent love, benevolent love has as its
foundation simply your good will. In other words, in benevolent love you're making the *intentional* choice to love people.
And why is that? Why does God call us to love others? First,
because He loves all people. Second, because all people are
made in His image.

Before I got married, I had been dating my then-girlfriend
Shale for many years. I had thought about marriage but could
never pull the trigger. I knew I loved her—that wasn't an issue. The issue was my love for her, many times, was based
on emotions. (Again, you need to have emotions in your love
for others, but it should not be based on emotions.) One day,
after speaking with my pastor about it, I realized I needed to
love her by choice. In other words, I needed to be intentional
about loving her no matter what happens in our relationship.

It wasn't but a month later that I proposed and we've now been married for almost four years.

In our witness we are to love people intentionally and genuinely. That means we can't say, "I say this because I love you," and then berate the person because they don't believe in Jesus. That's not love, but offensiveness. Jesus commands us to love sacrificially, even in evangelism. This could mean we sacrifice our egos in order to advance the conversation to the gospel. It could mean we not go in circles about a peripheral issue that the other person brought up. We are to love them. We are to share the gospel with them—the most loving thing we can do.

A SUPERNATURAL WITNESS

Only the Holy Spirit of God can make us into people who genuinely know the truth and genuinely love other people. The truth that grips our minds needs to penetrate down into the depths of our hearts and cling tightly. The truth we speak to lost people needs to come forth from a heart filled with love. The love we have for other people needs to be rooted in God's truth, which is in His Word.

This is the witness we need in our evangelism. Without truth and love, we either come off arrogantly (truth without love) or enabling somebody in his or her sin (love without truth). Truth with love is what it comes down to. To not have both means we are lopsided, immature Christians at best. At worst, it means we may need to be saved.

With all that being said—from chapter 1 to this sentence—we need to remember one crucial thing: obey the Great Commission.

•••

...

Conclusion:
Obey The Great Commission

...

Ponder this illustrative story by my late uncle, Keith Long, in his devotional *Room to Grow: Daily Thoughts for Men*:

"So, how are we going to work this?" I asked John Arrington as he drove to the house where we were to pick up two sisters for a double date. We were both sixteen and less than experienced at the dating game. And double dating seemed to create an extra problem for me.

"Work what?"

"I mean, should one of us go to the door, or both of us?"

"Hey, I know. Let's just pull up and honk," John said.

I pondered that possibility for just a moment. I'd seen other guys do it. Rather, I'd heard them do it. As it turned out, all my worry was for nothing. The girls were waiting at the door when we arrived. We didn't have to honk, we didn't have to go to the door, we didn't have to be introduced to their parents.

(Incidentally, their parents are some of the finest folks in the world. Only a sixteen-year-old could be afraid to meet them.)

I think of that incident now as I contemplate how Christian men approach people who are outside the fellowship of Jesus Christ. Do we park at the curb and honk? Do we expect them to come to us, and meet us on our terms?

Or do we get out of the car, go to the door, pay our respects, treat them with the same loving care that Christ did?

Too often, in my case, it's a matter of the former. I revert to acting like a spiritual sixteen-year-old. I want what seems easiest.

How about it? Are you waiting at the curb? Honking your horn? Staying in your comfort zone?[26]

ACTING LIKE SPIRITUAL SIXTEEN-YEAR-OLDS

Christians want what seems easiest. That's human nature. We struggle with engaging in evangelism. That struggle is natural because we know the message we possess is offensive and we are somewhat fearful of the reactions. But it's also because, like my late uncle said, many Christians are "spiritual sixteen-year-olds." We are so worried about what people think, so fearful about how unbelievers will react. Furthermore, we become *too* aware of our tone that we lose sight of the ultimate purpose: to proclaim the gospel of Jesus Christ that has saved us!

This whole book has been about ensuring that we are not distasteful in out witness. But as we've reached the conclusion, I want to talk about overcompensating. We don't want

[26] Keith Long, *Room to Grow: Daily Thoughts for Men* (Peabody: Hendrickson, 1999), 255.

to fear being offensive to the point that we no longer evange-lize. At that point, you're not offending the culture—you're offending God. And in some instances a bad witness that still gets the gospel across is better than no witness (Philippians 1:15-18).

It's a cop-out to say, "I shouldn't go out and witness be-cause I am prone to get too frustrated with people." That sim-ply isn't an excuse to not evangelize. If you're that concerned about your own shortcomings—which we all should be—than ask the Lord to replace your hard edges with soft ones.

GOD WILL SMOOTH OUT THE ROUGH SPOTS

God is not only in the business of justifying sinners but also sanctifying sinners (making them more like Jesus). Since this is true, you must trust that He will smooth out the rough edges in your life. It's good for you to be concerned about how you come across in your witness. Many Christians aren't concerned enough about that, and that's why this book was written. You are glorifying God by being vigilant about your sinful tendencies. What goes wrong, however, is if we say those rough spots mean we shouldn't evangelize. That trap can be just as easy to fall into.

I'm not sure where it originated, but the saying is undoubt-edly true: God uses crooked sticks to draw straight lines.

Just as you don't have to clean yourself up before you come to God (thank God for grace!), you likewise don't have to be perfectly holy in all areas in order to witness to the glory of the gospel (again, thank God for grace)! Do we believe this? If you had to wait to be a perfect Christian in order to witness, then it would never happen. All throughout Scripture we see God using imperfect humans to accomplish His perfect plan. From David (who was a murderer and adulterer) in the Old Testament to Peter (who denied Jesus three times) in the New Testament, there is no shortage of examples of God using sinful-yet-redeemed humans to further advance the kingdom of God through the proclamation of His gospel![27]

Are you fearful of witnessing—definitely when you think you might be too abrasive or insensitive? Remember what the latter part of the Great Commission tells us: Jesus will be with you until the end of the age. He isn't leaving you. He will be right beside you through the good and the bad witnesses. Don't rely on your own words, but the words the Spirit gives you (1 Corinthians 2:4). You will say offensive things on occasion, which is okay. You will slip up; you will fail. Don't be hard on yourself. Remember, the gospel is offensive. And when you become offensive as well—fess up to it. Show the person it's okay to admit our failures and sins. Don't worry so much about becoming offensive to the point that you become too timid in the conversation. When that happens, you begin to overthink things.

DON'T OVERTHINK EVANGELISM

I am an unashamed golfer. I know, I know, basically the whole world finds golf to be the most boring sport ever invented. I understand. But since I've been around the game my whole life, there's nothing boring about it. If you ever hit the perfect shot, then you will understand.

Ninety percent of golf is mental. Sure, you need to have good hand-eye coordination and you can't be clumsy. You need to know the ins and outs of the right way to swing, among other things. But above all else, you need to have a good "mental game." Part of having a good mental game is being able to have only one thought when you are about to hit the ball.

When I am over the ball, it's very tempting to be thinking about all the different things I need to do in order to hit a

---

[27] God also uses unredeemed humans to accomplish His perfect plans.

good shot. I need to widen my stance, make sure I keep my eye on the ball, and not forget to take the club straight back and straight through. Too many swing thoughts. Good golfers are able to have one thought over the ball. It doesn't have to be the same thought for each person, but it must be something. If your thoughts are jumbled over the ball, you will more than likely hit a poor shot. And then cue the yelling!

The same is true with witnessing to the gospel. If we approach conversations—whether on the street or over coffee—with too many thoughts in our head about how we should talk, we will become less focused on the message and more focused on the tone. That shouldn't be. Tone matters and makes a difference. But the biggest priority is making sure the gospel is communicated—rough edges and all! Have a singular mindset when talking to somebody about spiritual matters. You want to see this person come to Christ, right? Make sure the gospel is shared. Be aware of your tone, sure; be more aware of the message you intend to proclaim. God forbid you compromise the message just because you're focusing too much on your tone. Think of it this way: you don't want to walk on egg-shells but merely know they are there.

BEING OFFENSIVE

Friends, the gospel we preach is an offensive message. Why is that? It's offensive because it puts us in front of a mirror and says, "You're the problem." But, as we all know, there is a solution! That solution is Jesus Christ, our substitute.

The reason God didn't pluck us up into heaven when He saved us was to have us be the means of advancing the gospel all around the world. The Great Commission is a pleasure, not a burden. We should be aware of our tendency to be abrasive or rude. Christians should make it a point to be gentle in all conversations. You can be gentle and bold at the same time—Jesus was. The gospel we preach, the gospel we heard, the gospel that saved us—it's offensive to the unbelieving world. And it always will be.

But that doesn't mean we should be offensive, too.

Christian, trust Christ in all things. You trust Him for salvation; now trust Him in the work of evangelism. Trust that He will continue to transform your heart that makes for an effective witness to the gospel.

I know we all want to hear those beautiful words when we stand before Jesus one day:

"Well done, my good and faithful servant."

•••

...

Appendix:
What is the Gospel?

...

The gospel is so simple that a five-year-old can comprehend it, yet so complex that even the most learned theologians could explore the depths of it and never reach the bottom. What is this gospel? To sum it up precisely: the gospel is not a thing or an idea. The gospel is a person—Jesus Christ. The gospel is the person and work of Christ.

We all know what happened in the Garden of Eden, don't we? Even most unbelievers have knowledge of the opening pages of Genesis. Eve was tempted by the serpent (Satan) and succumbed to the temptation and ate the forbidden fruit. Adam ate as well. It was in that moment that they disobeyed God and their eyes were open and saw they were naked.

They had directly rebelled against their Creator.

As a result, all people are born into sin that they inherit through Adam. We are not born good people; we are not inherently righteous as some might say. We are, as Romans 3 tells us, not very good people. Wicked, actually. And in our wickedness we were headed straight for justice. We would receive justice from the wrath of God in hell for all eternity because we had sinned against a holy, righteous, and good God.

BUT GOD

Despite our rebellion, God sent Jesus into our world to be our substitute. Jesus was no mere man. He was also God. He was truly man, truly God. He was just as human as we are yet never ceased to also be the Creator of the universe, God in the flesh.

Moreover, Jesus did two amazing things on the sinner's behalf. He not only lived the life you couldn't live, but also died the death you deserved. You see, we are told in Scripture that, in order to make it to heaven, we must be perfectly righteous. No spot, blemish, or stain. Yet, if we're all honest with each other, we know that's impossible for a human to do because of our sin. But that's where Jesus comes in.

A SINLESS LIFE

Like I said above, Jesus lived the life you couldn't live and died the death you deserve. Jesus not only had to die on our behalf but also had to live a sinless life. Did you hear that, friend? Jesus never sinned on earth. He was perfect. Never did anything displeasing to his Father. He was perfect in every situation. He never sinned even while flipping tables in the temple. He was righteously indignant.

Where we fall woefully short, Jesus meets the perfect standards of a holy God. He dotted every "i" and crossed every "t." He never missed a beat—and the best part is this: *He did it all for you.* It was a key part of His mission on earth to live a sinless, spotless, righteous life for your sake.

But He didn't just live for you. He died for you.

WRATH-ABSORBING DEATH

Romans 6:23 says this: "For the wages of sin is death." In order for Christ to fulfill His mission faithfully, He had to die.

Blood had to be shed. Death is the result of sin—this is why we face death every day and have friends and family who die. It's the most awful thing in the world. It brings corruption and decay. It brings . . . death. But Jesus didn't merely die, friends. Jesus absorbed the full, unadulterated wrath of God.

In the garden of Gethsemane, Jesus was in great distress. At one point, the Bible tells us that He was sweating blood—all the while His disciples were asleep. He wasn't merely in anguish over the horrific death He was about to endure but knew He would be suffering much more than mere death: He would be absorbing the full wrath of the Father. On the cross—for you!

SOMEBODY IS PAYING THE PENALTY

Jesus lived and died so you may have eternal life. God loves you *that* much (John 3:16). But understand something: the penalty for your sin is either going to be paid by Jesus at the cross or by you in hell. You have the responsibility *today* to repent of your sins—to make an about-turn—and believe in the gospel (Mark 1:15). Repentance, though it may be largely neglected in evangelical circles today, is essential for salvation. One must repent in order to be saved. You must turn from your sin. Jesus literally commands you to repent—to turn away from godless idols to walk to the living God (1 Thessalonians 1:9). That is the essence of repentance. Embedded within repentance is the changing of one's mind. When you repent, you are changing your mind about sin, God, and the gospel. You go from loving sin to hating sin; you go from hating God to loving God. You go from not believing in the gospel to cherishing the gospel. You go from a child of Satan to a child of God.

And it's all by the grace of God (Ephesians 2:8–9). You cannot boast. The repentance and faith you exercised are both gifts from God. They were not yours. God gave them to you.

Of course, you made the active choice to do so, but only because God opened your heart to the beauty of Himself! That is grace, my friends, because you can't save yourself. None of us can. Other religions and cults try to tell you that you can appease God with your own works. That's utter nonsense. The Bible may paint a dark picture about your nature, but it's a realistic picture. And then God comes in to redeem the picture when He didn't have to! O, what a glorious God we serve!

HIS RIGHTEOUSNESS FOR YOUR SIN

Friends, we know Jesus saves, but do we know how it actually happens? It's a transaction of sorts. It's truly amazing to ponder.

When a person repents of their sin and believes in the person and work of Jesus Christ, all their sin—past, present, and future—is laid upon Jesus at the cross (this is why He was bearing the full weight of God's wrath—because He was carrying your sin). In turn, His perfect righteousness that He displayed in His life is transferred to you. This is called double imputation, and it is at the heart of the gospel. Because of this, not only are your sins forgiven, but also you are now perfectly righteous in God's sight—because of Jesus!

If there's ever a reason to rejoice, it's for this reality: that as a justified sinner, when God looks at you in all your filth, He sees Christ. Though you still sin, He sees perfection—a perfection that is not yours but has been given to you.

And it all comes back to grace. Undeserved merit granted by God because He loves us. He didn't condescend to earth, live a righteous life, and die a gruesome death because you're so lovable. No, He did those things because of His own glory. God is about His glory. There's only one person that should be about Himself in this world and it's God—because He made everything. From the galaxy to the tiniest insect—everything is His. His glory is rightfully shown in the salvation of sinners. His glory is also shown in the damnation of sinners who don't turn from their sin and believe in the One He sent.

HAVE YOU BEEN SAVED?

Friend, have you repented of your sin and believed in the gospel? If not, today is the day. Eternity is on the line. Hell is real and all who do not trust in Christ's finished work will be in hell for all eternity, bearing the full, never-ending brunt of God's wrath. That is what awaits sinners who stay in their sin.

But for those who swallow their pride, for those who turn from all their sin and make a dash for Christ, glory awaits them on the other side. Eternal life: no more tears, sorrow, or pain. Only joy, peace, fellowship, and the worship of the one true God forever.

Repent and believe.

•••

BIBLIOGRAPHY

•••

Albert Mohler, *We Cannot Be Silent: Speaking truth to a culture redefining sex, marriage, & the very reason of right and wrong* (Nashville, TN: Thomas Nelson, 2015), 138.

Trip Lee, "Don't Be a Jerk When the World Doesn't Like You," Desiring God, May 19, 2015, https://www.desiringgod.org/interviews/dont-be-a-jerk-when-the-world-doesnt-like-you.

Read Mercer Schuchardt, "8 Theses on Christianity and Twitter," Crossway, March 21, 2018, https://www.crossway.org/articles/8-theses-on-christians-and-twitter/.

Kevin DeYoung, "Distinguishing Marks of a Quarrelsome Person," The Gospel Coalition, June 13, 2019, https://www.thegospelcoalition.org/blogs/kevin-deyoung/distinguishing-marks-quarrelsome-person/.

Apologia Studios, "Pastor vs. Moral Nihilist," November 13, 2019, https://www.youtube.com/watch?v=UciOzJFTjc8.

Tony Miano, Crossencountersmin.com

Hillary Hanson, "Some Christians Are Extremely Unhappy About Starbucks' New Holiday Cups," Huffington Post, November 8, 2015, https://www.huffpost.com/entry/starbucks-red-cup-christmas-holiday-controversy_n_563f6e8fe4b0411d30715b15.

Gavin Ortlund, *Finding the Right Hills to Die On: The Case for Theological Triage* (Wheaton: Crossway, 2020) 18.

J. Gresham Machen, *Christianity and Liberalism*, new ed. (Grand Rapids: Eerdmans 2009) 2.

Diana Chandler, "Lifeway Pulls Hatmaker Books Over LGBT Views," Baptist Press, October 27, 2016, https://www.baptistpress.com/resource-library/news/lifeway-pulls-hatmaker-books-over-lgbt-views/.

Guy Prentiss Waters, *The Life and Theology of Paul* (Sanford: Reformation Trust, 2017) 3.

@RCSproul (RC Sproul), "We are not sinners because we sin. We sin because we are sinners." Twitter. 3 October 2017, 11:18 AM. https://twitter.com/RCSproul/status/915249707974365184

Steven Lawson, *The Moment of Truth* (Sanford: Reformation Trust, 2018) 9-16.

Keith Long, *Room to Grow: Daily Thoughts for Men* (Peabody: Hendrickson Publishers, 1999) 255.